# CROATIA

**SPIRAL**GUIDE

**AA** Publishing

# Contents

Written by Tony Kelly
Revised and updated by James Stewart

Project Editor Alison Cooke
Series Editor Karen Rigden
Series Designer Catherine Murray

Published by AA Publishing, a trading name of AA Media Limited,
whose registered office is Fanum House, Basing View, Basingstoke,
Hampshire, RG21 4EA. Registered number 06112600.

ISBN: 978-0-7495-6238-0

A CIP catalogue record for this book is available from the
British Library.

© AA Media Limited 2006, 2008, 2009
Maps © AA Media Limited 2006, 2008, 2009
New edition 2009

Cover design and binding style by permission of AA Publishing
Colour separation by Keenes, Andover
Printed and bound in China by Leo Paper Products

Find out more about AA Publishing and the wide range of travel
publications and services the AA provides by visiting our website at
www.theAA.com/bookshop

A03805
Maps in this title produced from map data supplied by Global
Mapping, Brackley, UK © Global Mapping/Hibernia
Transport map © Communicarta Ltd, UK

# The Magazine

A great holiday is more than just lying on a beach or shopping till you drop — to really get the most from your trip you need to know what makes the place tick. The Magazine provides an entertaining overview to some of the social, cultural and natural elements that make up the unique character of this engaging country.

# 1,001 DALMATIANS
## Island-hopping in the Adriatic

**With more than 1,000 islands to explore, the cleanest seas in the Mediterranean, no tide to worry about and benign weather conditions, it is no wonder that sailors love the Croatian coast. In the last deacde, Croatia has emerged as a serious rival to Greece and Turkey as the Mediterranean's top sailing destination.**

In recent years long-standing yachtie destinations such as Hvar Town and Dubrovnik have received a glossy makeover to create glamorous alternatives to the French Riviera where café-culture rules and a fashionable bar scene swings in summer. Elsewhere, numberless hidden coves – and some of Croatia's most escapist beaches – await those who can get afloat. And then there is the simple joy of supper in a waterside *konoba* (inn), perhaps a *rakija digestif*, before you return to a yacht moored in a moonlit harbour far off the tourist trail.

### Island-hopping
There are three ways of island-hopping in the Adriatic. One is to use the excellent network of ferries, most of them run by Jadrolinija (► 36), which links the ports of Zadar, Split and Dubrovnik to the major inhabited islands. Another is to sign aboard a traditional gulet motor-sailer, which usually spends a week cruising between the islands. The other is to take your own boat. You can charter yachts locally, or arrange it in advance (see panel opposite). The basic choice is between a bareboat charter, where at least one member of the crew must be an experienced sailor, and a skippered boat, where you can help with the sailing, but pay extra for a captain in charge. Some operators also offer full-service yachts, complete with a captain,

---

### FACTS AND FIGURES

- 1,185 islands, about 50 of which are inhabited
- 5,835km (3,625 miles) of coastline
- 4,058km (2,522 miles) of which is on islands
- 50 marinas
- 350 natural harbours
- 13,000 berths

Page 5: Yacht off the coast of one of the Korati Islands
Above: Dubrovnick harbour, packed with boats

cook, steward and hostess. Another alternative is to join a flotilla, where you have to be able to sail your own boat, but are part of a larger party where expert help is available if required.

In your own yacht, you can choose where to stop, perhaps mooring one night in a chic waterside town and the next in a deserted bay. Most of the 50 marinas are open all year and are all within a day's sailing of each other. For a real back-to-nature experience, head for the uninhabited islands of the Kornati archipelago near Zadar. Just look out for the bora, a strong northeasterly wind that blows from the mainland to the sea.

## USEFUL WEBSITES

- Ferry routes and timetables: www.jadrolinija.hr
- Operators of 21 marinas: www.aci-club.hr
- Adriatic Yacht Charter: www.ayc.hr
- Yacht charter: www.clubadriatic.com
- Croatian tourist board, with full list of marinas and yacht charters: www.croatia.hr
- Bareboat and skippered charters: www.sailcroatia.net
- Flotilla holidays: www.sailingholidays.com
- UK tour operator with gulet cruises from Opatija, Split and Durbovnik: www.bosmeretravel.co.uk

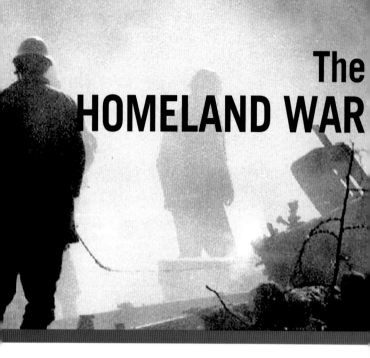

# The HOMELAND WAR

**Just off the courtyard of the Sponza Palace in Dubrovnik is a memorial room to the victims of the 1991–2 siege. To many visitors, the photos of dead teenagers, shattered buildings and the torn remnants of a Croatian flag from Mount Srdj provide a shocking reminder of the realities of war.**

### A Young Country

Stay in one of the buzzing coastal resorts in summer and you could be forgiven for forgetting the most important fact about Croatia – that this is a young country, born out of the former Yugoslavia and still recovering from the wars that tore it apart little over a decade ago. Head inland to Vukovar, or the Serb villages around Knin, and the scars of war are there for all to see in the burned-out houses and pockmarked facades. The emotional damage is less visible, but it exists all the same. The few Croats and Serbs who remain in these areas share an uneasy peace, leading separate lives, drinking in separate bars and sending their children to separate schools.

### Look to the Future

In many ways, Croatia is still in denial about what it calls the Homeland War. The first national war memorial opened in 2006 at Zagreb's Mirogoj Cemetery, replacing a pile of bricks erected on a street corner by families of the victims. Most politicians prefer to focus on the future, portraying Croatia as a modern, forward-looking European nation. But the world

**Serbian soldiers shell Croatian targets, 9 February, 1993**

is not so easily convinced. Talks on entry to the European Union were held up in 2005 over Croatia's inability or unwillingness to track down fugitive generals wanted by the international war crimes tribunal in The Hague. Many of the soldiers accused of war crimes are still regarded as heroes in Croatia.

"Many of the soldiers accused of war crimes are still regarded as heroes in Croatia"

## End of an Era

In hindsight, the wars of 1991–5 were an inevitable consequence of the break-up of Yugoslavia. The country had been held together by President Tito (1892–1980), a Croatian Communist fighter who came to power in 1945 after leading the Partisan resistance movement against both the Ustaše puppet regime of Croatia and the royalist Serbian Chetniks during World War II. For 35 years, Tito managed to unite the various people of the Balkans – Croats, Serbs, Slovenians, Macedonians, Bosnians, Albanians and others – behind his own brand of socialism, rejecting both Western-style democracy and Soviet-style Communism, and combining the methods of dictatorship with large elements of personal freedom.

Ten years after Tito's death, Yugoslavia fell apart. Croatia declared independence in 1991 and was attacked by units of the Yugoslav People's Army (JNA), a largely pro-Serb military based in Belgrade. On the pretext of protecting the Serbian minority in Croatia, Yugoslav forces started to move into Serb-populated villages, establishing the Republic of the Serbian Krajina at Knin. Before long, the Serbs controlled a third of Croatia, cutting off road and rail links from Zagreb

## "Croatia stands at the crossroads of cultures"

to Split and evicting Croats from their homes in a practice which came to be known as "ethnic cleansing". When Operation Storm ended the Serbian occupation in 1995, most Serbs fled into Bosnia. Although the war officially ended in 1995, parts of eastern Slavonia were not returned to Croatia until 1998.

Croatia's war leader was Franjo Tuđman (1922–99), a former Yugoslav general who became a hard-line Croatian nationalist and the first president of independent Croatia. His successor, Stjepan Mesić, has instead adopted a much more liberal, pro-Western attitude, negotiating with the European Union and co-operating with the war crimes tribunal. In 2005, he was elected to serve a second five-year term and that October he delivered up Operation Storm mastermind General Ante Gotovina to The Hague to stand trial for war crimes. However, a poll after the arrest found that 60 per cent of the country thought Gotovina was not guilty.

### Balkan is a Dirty Word

Most people have traditionally referred to the Yugoslav states as part of the Balkan peninsula, but these days Balkan is a dirty word. Political leaders repeatedly call Croatia a Central European nation. In truth, Croatia stands at the crossroads of cultures. Torn for centuries between Venice and Istanbul, Catholic and Orthodox, it is no surprise that Croatia and Serbia were the catalysts for the worst war in Europe since 1945.

**From left: President Tito (1892–1980). Memorial to all those who died in the 1990s war along the bank of the river Danube. War damaged buildings in Vukovar.**

## TIME LINE

**c600 BC**
Greeks establish settlements on Adriatic coast, followed later by the Romans.

**7th century AD**
Slav tribes of Serbs and Croats migrate to Balkans.

**925**
Tomislav becomes first Croatian king.

**1094**
Founding of Zagreb.

**1102**
Croatia becomes part of Hungary.

**14th century AD**
Rise of Venetian power in Adriatic. Founding of republic of Ragusa at Dubrovnik.
For the next few centuries, Croatia is fought over by Austro-Hungarian, Venetian and Turkish-Ottoman empires.

**1527–1918**
Period of Habsburg (Austro-Hungarian) rule throughout most of Croatia, excluding Dalmatia.

**1918**
Croatia enters Kingdom of the Serbs, Croats and Slovenes, later Yugoslavia.

**1941–45**
Nazi puppet government known as Ustaše takes power in Croatia; Tito organizes partisan resistance throughout Yugoslavia.

**1945–80**
Communist rule under Tito.

**1990**
Franjo Tuđman wins multi-party elections.

**1991**
Croatia declares independence. War breaks out with sieges of Dubrovnik and Vukovar.

**1995**
Erdut agreement ends war with Serbia.

**2000**
Stjepan Mesić elected president.

**2003**
Ivo Sanader of Tuđman's HDZ (Croatian Democratic Union) becomes prime minister.

**2005**
Croatia starts entry talks with EU. Croatian general Ante Gotovina is arrested on allegations of war crimes.

**2010**
Proposed entry date into the EU.

# NATURISM

## THE NAKED TRUTH

**As the tour boats enter the mouth of the Limski Kanal, the passengers on board take out their cameras and binoculars to admire the view. Some of them get rather more than they were expecting, for this is the site of the biggest naturist colony in Europe.**

The tradition of nude sunbathing in Croatia goes back a while. The first official naturist beach opened on Rab in 1934. Two years later, the British king Edward VIII and his lover Wallis Simpson asked permission to swim naked in Kandarola Bay. Croatia has had a laid-back attitude to nudity ever since.

### Embracing the Culture

While other countries tolerated nudism and confined it to out-of-the-way places, Croatia wholeheartedly embraced it, opening Europe's first commercial naturist resorts in the 1960s. Koversada, which began in 1961 on a small islet off Vrsar, has grown into a mega-resort, with space for 7,000 people staying in campsites, bungalows and apartments. There are restaurants, shops, children's playgrounds, tennis courts, mini-golf, beach volleyball and sailing boats for rent. This is merely the biggest of some 30 official naturist resorts, many of them in Istria.

You can dress as nature intended at hundreds of remote beaches and coves on the Adriatic islands and coast. As a general rule, the further you go off the beaten track, the more acceptable nudity becomes. Ask around at any busy harbour in summer and you will find boats willing to take you to FKK (*freikörperkultur* or "free body culture") beaches on nearby islands. Even at mainstream beaches, there is usually a section where nudity is tolerated.

The distinction between naturists and "textiles" (people who wear clothes) in Croatia is gradually breaking down. Around ten per cent of all visitors to Croatia sunbathe naked at some point, and topless female bathing is the norm. In the past, FKK beaches were strictly for naturists but these days "clothing optional" is the rule. If you do visit a nudist beach and decide to keep your clothes on, just remember that staring is rude and photography is definitely out. Remember, if you take your clothes off – don't forget the sunblock.

### What is Naturism?

Naturism is defined by the International Naturist Federation as "a way of living in harmony with nature, characterized by the practice of communal nudity". It is not to be confused with sex or eroticism – as any visit to a naturist beach will quickly confirm. You can find more information on naturism in Croatia on the Croatia Naturally website at www.cronatur.com.

**With a relaxed attitude to nudity, Croatia has a number of beautiful nudist beaches**

# THE
# BEST OF
# CROATIA

Even on a short break you can enjoy the
delights and charms of this unique country.
To help you get the most of your visit, here
is a selection Croatia's best experiences.

## Ten Special Experiences
- A walk around Dubrovnik's city walls (► 148).
- The view of Rovinj on the boat trip from Crveni Otok (► 98).
- Joining the evening *korzo* to see the beautiful people of Zagreb (► 47).
- Walking among lakes and waterfalls in the Plitvička Jezera (► 70–72) or Krka (► 118–119) national parks.
- Sitting on the deck of the early-morning ferry from Split to one of the Adriatic islands.
- Sipping Prošek (sweet red wine) on a summer evening by the sea.
- Taking in a concert at the Roman amphitheatre in Pula (► 112).
- Getting away from it all on a farm in the Zagorje (► 86) or Lonjsko Polje (► 85).
- Cruising through the uninhabited islands of the Kornati archipelago (► 134).
- Taking off your clothes and getting back to nature on one of Croatia's many naturist beaches (► 12–13).

## Best Hotels
- Pucić Palace, Dubrovnik (► 158).
- Villa Dubrovnik, Dubrovnik (► 159).
- Villa Angelo d'Oro, Rovinj (► 109).
- Mozart, Opatija (► 108).
- Livadić, Samobor (► 86).

## Ten Things To Taste While You're Here
- *Pršut*: cured ham from Istria or Dalmatia, similar to an Italian prosciutto.
- *Paški sir*: strong sheep's cheese from the island of Pag.
- *Čevapčići*: popular snack of grilled meat rissoles, served with raw onions, bread and *ajvar* (aubergine and pepper relish).
- *Crni rižot*: black risotto, coloured with cuttlefish ink.
- *Brudet*: Dalmatian fish stew.
- *Pasticada*: Dalmatian dish of veal cooked in sweet wine.
- Truffles from Istria.
- Oysters from Ston.
- Dingač red wine from the Pelješac peninsula.
- *Biska* (mistletoe brandy) from Istria.

## Best Beaches
- Zlatni Rat on the island of Brač is a stunning shingle spit backed by pine woods (► 127).
- Beaches along the Makarska Rivijera offer a mix of sand and pebbles and are suitable for children (► 136).

There are good sandy beaches at:
- Baška, on the southern tip of the island of Krk, in Kvarner Bay, (► 107).
- Sabunike, just north of the town of Nin (► 133).
- Lovrečina, near Postira, on the north coast of the island of Brač (► 128).
- Saplunara, on the southern tip of the island of Mljet (► 151).
- Prižna, at Lumbarda on the island of Korčula (► 154).
- Šunj, at Lopud on the relaxed Elafiti Islands (► 157).
- Lopar, on the island of Rab, the most inviting island in Kvarner Bay (► 107).

Take a dip in the pool at the Skradinski Buk waterfalls in the Krka National Park

# STAYING ON THE
# **FARM**

**Croatia promotes itself as "the Mediterranean as it used to be" and there's no better way to sample timeless traditional lifestyles than to take advantage of the growing trend towards rural tourism – all the reason you need to explore away from the coast.**

In the old days, visitors to Croatia stayed in one of the big package hotels on the seafront, spending their days on the beaches and their nights in the hotel bar, seeing very little of Croatia beyond their chosen resort. When tourism collapsed as a result of the 1991–5 war, the local people decided to take a fresh look. These days, the buzzwords are "rural tourism" as more and more people return to their roots and open their houses to a new wave of adventurous visitors.

### A Breath of Fresh Air
Agrotourism is breathing new life into rural Croatia. Old villages which were almost abandoned are being repopulated by a younger generation, eager

Lush countryside surrounds Motovun and the other hill towns of inland Istria to restore dilapidated stone farmhouses and develop organic agriculture. Driving through the inland regions, you come across roadside signs advertising *agroturizam, seoski turizam* or *seljački turizam*, which all mean much the same thing. It could be a stone cottage with a couple of spare rooms, or a grand farmhouse that has been turned into a luxury rural hotel, complete with a swimming pool in the grounds.

## Leading the Way

Istria is where agrotourism is at its most developed, helped by the local tourist authorities who have set up wine and olive oil routes and bicycle trails to encourage visitors inland. A booklet of farmstays, available at tourist offices, is published each year and the website lists over 200 properties (www.istra.com/agroturizam).

With its olive groves, vineyards and Tuscan-style hill towns, Istria makes the perfect agrotourism destination, especially as the sea is never far away. After an afternoon on the beach, what could be better than to return to your cosy farmhouse for a delicious home-cooked meal of fresh local produce, accompanied by the farmer's own wine and a welcome glass of herb brandy?

## Agrotourism is Taking Off

Other areas where agrotourism is becoming popular include the Zagorje, north of Zagreb; the villages around the Plitvice Lakes; and the Baranja region of northeast Slavonia, near the Kopački Rit wetlands. You will also find examples of rural tourism on some of the larger islands, such as Korčula and Hvar. Some places offer horseback-riding and bicycles for

**Traditional wooden farmhouse in Lonjsko Polje National Park**

rent; others will let you join in with everything from feeding the animals to picking grapes and searching for wild mushrooms. Facilities vary, but what they all share is the chance for an insight into rural life.

## Alternative Accommodation

If you really want to get away from it all, you could stay in a lighthouse on the Adriatic coast. Eleven of them have been converted into apartments, sleeping between two and eight people. All apartments have electricity or gas, hot and cold water, TV and a kitchen, though you will have to take your own provisions for the week. Three of the lighthouses – at Makarska, Poreč and Savudrija – are on the mainland close to restaurants and shops; the one at Savudrija, on Istria's northern tip, is the oldest in Croatia, built in 1818. The others are all on islands, with varying degrees of isolation. The lighthouse at Palagruža, built in 1875, stands 90m (295 feet) above the sea on the remotest island in the Adriatic, 70km (43 miles) from Vis and halfway between the Croatian and Italian coasts. The island is 1,400m (4,590 feet) long and 300m (985 feet) wide, with its own beach and excellent fishing. Boat transfers can be arranged from Korčula or Split, but once there you are on your own. You can use your mobile phone to summon a boat or helicopter to the island in an emergency. There are two four-person apartments, and a resident lighthouse keeper for company. Just hope that you all get on with each other.

Further infomation on staying in a Croatian lighthouse can be found at www.lighthouses-croatia.com. Accommodation can also be booked through this website.

**Vineyard near Lumbarda on the Korčula Island**

# BUILDING BLOCKS OF A NATION

**Croatia's architectural diversity is a result of its history and has seen a number of influences, ranging from Venice to Vienna.**

## Roman

The Romans conquered the Adriatic coastline in the 1st century BC, establishing their province of Dalmatia and building cities at Pula and Zadar. The emperor Diocletian was born in the Dalmatian city of Salona in AD 245 and later built his retirement palace at Split.

### Highlights

- The arena at Pula (➤ 101).
- The Temple at Pula (➤ 102).
- Diocletian's Palace (➤ 123).

## Byzantine

After the Romans, Croatia was ruled by the Byzantine empire and Christianity became the main religion. The Slavic tribes from Ukraine adopted Christianity and built churches influenced by Greek, Latin and Celtic architecture.

### Highlights

- The mosaics in the Basilica of Euphrasius at Poreč (➤ 94–95).
- The Church of St Donat at Zadar (➤ 133).
- The Church of the Holy Cross at Nin (➤ 133).

From top: impressive peristyle court of Diocletian's Palace at Split; Croatian National Theatre in Zagreb; Gate of Hercules at Pula, the site of a historic Roman settlement

## Venetian

The finest buildings on the Dalmatian coast were constructed during the Venetian rule between the 14th and 18th centuries. Master architects such as Juraj Dalmatinac (George the Dalmatian; c1400–73) and Nikola Firentinac (Nicholas of Florence) employed a transitional style which has come to be known as Gothic-Renaissance. The Sponza Palace and Rector's Palace in Dubrovnik both symbolize this style. Most towns along the coast have Venetian-style loggias, usually adorned with the winged lion of St Mark, a symbol of Venice. Dubrovnik broke free from Venice in 1358, becoming the city-state of Ragusa, so the winged lion is conspicuously absent, though in other respects the architecture is similar. Much of Dubrovnik was destroyed in an earthquake in 1667 and the uniformity of the city today is due to the fact that it was all rebuilt at the same time.

**Highlights**
- Šibenik Cathedral (➤ 134–135).
- Trogir Cathedral (➤ 120–122).
- The arsenal and theatre at Hvar (➤ 130).

## Baroque

The extravagant baroque style, characterized by its ornate, brightly coloured facades, was popular in northern Croatia during the 18th century as a symbol of Catholicism on the borders of the Ottoman empire. The Baroque style reached its peak in the town of Varaždin, which was briefly the capital of Croatia.

**Highlights**
- The town centre at Varaždin (➤ 76–77).
- The Tvrđa at Osijek (➤ 83).
- The Eltz Palace at Vukovar (➤ 83–84).

### The 19th Century
The end of the Habsburg era was marked by grandiose public buildings combining elements of classical, Gothic, Renaissance and baroque styles. The best examples of which can be seen in Zagreb's Donji Grad, the Lower Town.

### Highlights
- Trg Bana Jelačića, Zagreb (➤ 46–48).
- Croatian National Theatre, Zagreb (➤ 64).
- The seafront villas and promenade at Opatija (➤ 104–105).

## Dubrovnik's Walls
The restoration of Dubrovnik's city walls is one of the great success stories of modern Croatia. During the siege of 1991–2, they were repeatedly shelled and some of the citizens took refuge in the fortresses. Today, tourists once again stroll around the ramparts of this World Heritage city and there are few visible signs of damage. The walls date from the 15th century, at a time when the republic of Ragusa felt itself under threat from the growing Ottoman empire, following the fall of Constantinople in 1453. The main towers were the work of Michelozzo Michelozzi (1396–1472), chief architect to the Medici family of Florence; among others who worked on the walls was Juraj Dalmatinac, architect of Šibenik cathedral. Up to 25m (82 feet) high in places, and supported by two free-standing fortresses outside the Pile and Ploče gates, the walls were not breached until Napoleon's troops entered the city in 1806. Ironically, the attack on the walls in 1991 first drew international attention to the war in Croatia; after the war, money poured in for their restoration.

**This magnificent Roman amphitheatre at Pula is the sixth-largest in the world**

# RIVER DEEP, MOUNTAIN HIGH
## THE WILDS OF CROATIA

Mountains, lakes, rivers, waterfalls, forests, canyons and

a sparkling blue sea – if you want spectacular natural scenery, Croatia has it all.

About 40 per cent of the country is mountainous, with the rugged peaks and grey karst limestone of the Dinaric range providing a natural border with Bosnia and a dramatic backdrop to the Adriatic coast. The highest peak is Mount Dinara (1,831m/6,007 feet) near Knin. Carved through by gorges and riddled with underground rivers and caves, the Dinaric Mountains extend out to sea, their partially submerged

**Left: Paklenica National Park is a popular destination for rock-climbing. Below: Meandering paths of Plitvice National Park**

Above: Mountains of Paklenica National
Park. Right: Follow the footpaths round the
Zlanti Rat forest park in Rovinj

summits forming the barren islands
of Pag and the Kornati archipelago.
Another 30 per cent of Croatia is
covered in forests of oak, pine, fir,
beech and spruce.

Croatia has always been
passionate about preserving its
natural heritage. The first national
park was established in 1949 at the
Plitvice Lakes (➤ 70–72) . There
are now eight national parks where
wildlife is protected and tourism
carefully controlled (➤ 25). A
further ten nature parks include the
Kopački Rit (➤ 78–79), Lonjsko
Polje (➤ 80–81) flood plains and
Mount Medvednica (➤ 59) north
of Zagreb. Nature parks offer a
slightly lower level of protection and
access is generally free to visitors,
whereas there is a fee to enter the
national parks.

## Wildlife

As well as bears, other large
mammals which thrive in Croatia's
mountains and forests include lynx,
wolf and wild boar, all of which may
be seen in the Plitvice Lakes, North

**Croatia's National parks are home to Golden Eagles and European Brown bears**

Velebit and Risnjak national parks. Red and roe deer are also common, and mouflon, a wild mountain sheep, are found on the Biokovo massif, behind Makarska. Another common mammal is the pine marten, a weasel-like creature which feeds on small rodents and birds, that has even given its name (*kuna*) to the Croatian currency.

Birds of prey include golden eagles and peregrine falcons, particularly in the Paklenica and North Velebit mountain ranges, and a colony of griffon vultures on the island of Cres. White and black storks nest in the wetlands of northern Croatia in spring and summer, particularly in the Lonjsko Polje, where you may also see egrets, herons and cormorants.

Dolphins frequently swim off the Adriatic coast, and there is a school of around 200 bottle-nosed dolphins around the islands of Cres and Lošinj.

## The Great Outdoors

Croatia is a paradise for walkers, mountaineers, cyclists, canoeists, sailors, divers, extreme sports enthusiasts and anyone who appreciates the great outdoors. The tradition of mountaineering goes back a long way and the highland regions have an excellent network of well-marked paths and mountain huts. The lower slopes and forests are fine for gentle hiking, but the higher mountains are for serious climbers only. Even in summer, when

### NATIONAL PARKS

- Nacionalni Park Brijuni (➤ 99–100).
- Nacionalni Park Kornati (➤ 134).
- Nacionalni Park Krka (➤ 118–119).
- Nacionalni Park Mljet (➤ 150–151).
- Nacionalni Park Plitvička Jezera (➤ 70–72).
- Nacionalni Park Risnjak (➤ 105).

the coast is bathed in sunshine, there can be snow in the mountains. In winter, the mountain regions are bitterly cold, with sub-zero temperatures the norm. Anyone planning serious alpine walking should get hold of *Walking in Croatia* by Rudolf Abraham, published by Cicerone Press. For gentler walks, head for the Medvednica range north of Zagreb or the green hills of the Žumberak-Samoborsko Gorje.

> "Croatia has always been passionate about preserving its natural heritage"

Rock-climbers could try the challenging faces of the Paklenica and North Velebit national parks. Paklenica has more than 400 climbing routes for all levels of ability, including a steep rock wall at the entrance to the gorge for beginners. Alpine and free climbing is also possible on Brač, Mljet and Vis, and in Zlatni Rt forest park at Rovinj. Canoeing, kayaking and white-water rafting are all popular activities, with local companies offering excursions on the rivers Kupa, Dobra, Zrmanja and Cetina. Plus, rafting on the River Una, on the border of Bosnia and Croatia, can reach grades 4 and 5. The top rafting destination is Omiš, convenient for visitors to Makarska Rivijera or the Dalmatian islands.

### The Bear Facts

It is estimated that between 400 and 600 European brown bears live in the Gorski Kotar and Velebit mountain ranges, including the Plitvice Lakes and Risnjak national parks. The brown bear is the largest living land carnivore, weighing up to 300kg (660 lb). Despite being virtually extinct in other parts of Europe, bears can be legally hunted in Croatia outside the national parks and you may be surprised to find smoked bear meat and pâté on sale in smart restaurants and shops.

# Sword Dancers of
# KORČULA

**The sword dance is a regular feature of life on the island of Korčula and has become a popular tourist spectacle.**

So the story begins of the *Moreška*, a ritualized sword dance that arrived on the island of Korčula in the 16th century. The roots of the dance are lost in the mists of time, but its name derives from the Spanish or Italian word for 'Moorish' and it is a variation of the mock battles between Muslim and Christian soldiers which have been performed across the Mediterranean since the time of the Crusades. In Korčula, it was easily adapted to fit the local situation, at a time when the Venetian rulers of Dalmatia faced a constant threat from the Turkish Ottoman empire.

## The Story of the *Moreška*

A familiar tale of good versus evil and as always the good guys come out on top. It opens with the Black King, dressed in black, dragging a pretty Muslim maiden across the stage in chains as he attempts to persuade her to return his unrequited love. The woman, Bula, rejects him because of her love for Osman, the White King, who is confusingly dressed in red.

The sword dancers of Korčula put on a spectacular performance

Eventually the two kings bring on their armies of followers, also dressed in black and red, and the dance begins. To the accompaniment of a brass band, the two armies join battle, forming a circle as they act out the seven different movements of a highly stylized war dance, thrusting and clashing their swords in pairs. Each of the movements has its own rhythm; during the final

> "sword clashes are fast and furious and sparks fly through the air"

movement, the sword clashes are fast and furious and sparks fly through the air as the Black King's army retreats into the middle of an ever smaller circle before collapsing, dying and defeated, onto the ground. The Black King surrenders his sword and the White King frees Bula from her chains with a kiss as the audience bursts into applause.

## Moreška Revival

By the end of World War II, the *moreška* had almost died out and there were few people on Korčula who remembered the dance. It was revived by the local barber, schoolteacher, policeman and conductor of the town orchestra. These days, throughout July and August, a Festival of Sword Dances takes place across the island, with performances of *moreška* in Korčula town and the similar *kumpanija* dance in Blato, Smokvica and Vela Luka.

On Monday and Thursday evenings in summer, the Sveta Cecilija dance troupe performs the *moreška* on a special stage outside the Kopnena Vrata (Land Gate). You will probably be thankful that modern performance lasts 45 minutes, instead of the traditional two hours.

# CROATIA:
## A Menu of Diversity

**There are some constants to Croatian cuisine – such as Balkan hamburger *čevapčići*, *raznjići* pork kebabs, or the typically Adriatic obsession with charcoal-grilled steak. But you don't have to travel far to sample the culinary variety of a nation located where the Balkans meets Italy and central Europe meets the Mediterranean.**

For most visitors, Croatian menus will be coastal, epitomized by the diet from Dalmatia, specializing in classic Mediterranean fish and seafood which is fresh and unfussy, grilled over charcoal or baked in a salt-crust, then seasoned with a splash of olive oil and a lemon wedge. Alternatives are *buzaru* dishes, a rich pot of seafood prepared with tomato and white wine, or local *bouillabase brodet*. The traditional meat main course is *pašticada*, a stew of beef in sweet wine, or spit-roast lamb is superb on sheep-rearing Kavarner islands such as Pag or Creš. The typical side dish is *blitve*, a medley of Swiss chard and potates with garlic.

### SIX OF THE BEST

Recent years have seen the nation's master-chefs bring gourmet twists to classic dishes. Names on any self-respecting foodie's check-list include:

- **Toklarija** (► 110): first-class Istrian slow-food in a rustic-chic setting.
- **Valsabbion** (► 111): a slick restaurant whose daring combinations are often lauded as the finest in Istria.
- **Zigante** (► 110): the flagship of a regional chain founded by the finder of the world's largest truffle.
- **Le Mandrač** (► 111): Asian-nuanced fusion food served in a glamorous glass-skinned dining room.
- **Zlatna Školjka** (► 139): rabbit with figs is typical of this award-winning slow-food restaurant on Hvar.
- **Kapetanova Kuča** (► 161): harbourfront restaurant famous for its oysters farmed in Mali Ston.

**A delicious Croatian spread includes Istrian prosciutto**

However, the all-Dalmatian dish is that prepared under a *peka*, a metal lid that covers the food and is heaped with charcoals. Whether lamb, veal or octopus, this is slow food at its best; cooked with sinew and fat to provide a dish that is as succulent as it is flavoursome. Many chefs often request advance notice to prepare a *peka* dish, but it's worth it for a taste of a regional speciality barely changed for 2,000 years.

## Essential Flavours

While centuries under Venetian rule have left Dalmatian menus littered with risottos and pasta, the Italian influence is strongest in Istria. The best European foodie destination no-one knows, this northern region has a palate as Italian as its dialect; rustic Italian bean-and-vegetable soup *manestra* or homemade *kobasice* (sausages), pastas such as *fuži* (fusilli) and *njoki* (gnocchi). This is also the state which prides itself on prosciutto-style *pršut* ham and especially white and black truffles (*tartufi*), which are rooted out around Motovun every autumn by crack man-and-dog teams.

Landlocked contintental Croatia has more robust tastes, with a palate for produce from its farms and neighbours. In the Zagorje north of Zagreb, you'll find turkey (*purica*), endless varieties of cabbage and *štruckli* like miniature dumplings, filled and often filled with cottage cheese. Slavonia, like adjacent Hungary, prefers its dishes spicy – paprika is sprinkled liberally on most plates and adds a piquant bite to *kulen* salami or spicy *čobanac* stew. However, a local speciality in the far east of Croatia is carp roasted on a stick.

# FOOTBALL CRAZY

**For a country with 4.5 million people, Croatia has enjoyed remarkable sporting success with an impressive squad that scores far above its size.**

After it was recognised by FIFA and UEFA in 1992, the team made the grade for every major competition except Euro 2000 since its debut in Euro 1996, and finished third in the World Cup 1998, no disgrace since it was beaten by eventual winner France.

Regional pride goes to Dinamo Zagreb (www.nk-dinamo.hr) and Hajduk Split (www.hnkhajduk.hr). Fierce rivals, the clubs have monpolised the top spot every year since the formation of the Prva HNL domestic league in 1992, and are the only Croatian league clubs to have played in Europe's Champions League tournament. Dinamo have the edge in silverware, with ten titles to Hajduk's six as of 2008.

A match at the 40,000-seater Maksimir stadium (► 64) in Zagreb or Split's 35,000-capacity Poljud stadium is a must for any footie fan. Games are usually played at weekends in a domestic season that runs from mid-August to late-May, with a two-month break from January. Tickets for games can be picked up at the gates of both stadiums, east and north of the city centres respectively, for as little as 30kn. International games are usually played in Zagreb and advanced ticket purchases are a must.

**A clash between Dinamo and Basel in Zagreb, during the UEFA Championship**

# Finding Your Feet

# First Two Hours

Croatia is an easy destination to get to; bordering a number of European countries makes travelling by car and train relatively easy. Lying on the Adriatic coast also makes arriving by sea possible; however, the most popular choice of travel is by air to one of Croatia's many airports dotted around the country.

## Arriving by Air

Croatia's main international airport is at Zagreb, with regular flights on Croatia Airlines to all major European capitals. In summer, most visitors fly directly to one of the coastal airports at Dubrovnik, Split, Zadar, Rijeka and Pula.

## Zagreb

- Zagreb airport is at **Pleso**, 17km (10.5 miles) south of the city.
- **Facilities in the arrivals hall** include a bank, ATMs (cash machines), post office and car-rental agencies.
- Croatia Airlines' **shuttle buses** run once or twice an hour to a terminal beside the bus station in Zagreb. The journey takes 30 minutes and tickets (30kn) can be bought on the bus. From the bus station, it is a 20-minute walk to central Zagreb, or tram No 6 runs directly to the main square, Trg Bana Jelačića.
- A **taxi to central Zagreb** from outside the arrivals hall will cost around 200kn–250kn.

## Dubrovnik

- Dubrovnik airport is at **Čilipi**, 20km (12 miles) south of the city, near Cavtat.
- **Facilities in the arrivals hall** include a bank, ATMs (cash machines), post office and car-rental agencies.
- Atlas **shuttle buses** drop passengers at the bus station and outside the Pile Gate for access to the old city; note that return journeys to the airport do not stop at Pile Gate. The journey takes 30 minutes and tickets (35kn) can be bought on the bus.
- **Taxis cost** around 200kn to take you to the centre of Dubrovnik and 100kn to Cavtat.

## Split

- Split airport is at **Kaštela**, 25km (15.5 miles) west of the city near the old town of Trogir.
- **Facilities in the arrivals hall** include a bank, ATMs (cash machines), post office and car-rental agencies.
- Croatia Airlines' **shuttle buses** drop passengers on the waterfront Riva. The journey takes 30 minutes and tickets (30kn) can be bought on the bus.
- A **taxi to central Split** costs around 200kn–250kn.

## Airport Information

**Zagreb**: 01 4562 222; www.zagreb-airport.hr
**Dubrovnik**: 020 773 100; www.airport-dubrovnik.hr
**Split**: 021 203 555; www.split-airport.hr
**Zadar**: 023 205 800; www.zadar-airport.hr
**Rijeka**: 051 842 132; www.rijeka-airport.hr
**Pula**: 052 530 105; www.airport-pula.hr

## Arriving by Land

- There are **border crossings** with Slovenia, Hungary, Bosnia-Hercegovina, Serbia and Montenegro.
- Visitors **arriving from Italy** must pass briefly through Slovenia on their way into Croatia.
- **Citizens of EU countries** entering via Hungary and Slovenia will face minimal formalities at the border.
- If you are **bringing your own car**, you will need to show a valid driving licence, insurance papers and registration or ownership documents. If you have rented a car in another country, you must be sure to get the rental documents stamped to confirm that your vehicle insurance is valid in Croatia.
- **Buses from European destinations** arrive at the main bus station in Zagreb. Central Zagreb is a 20-minute walk or a short ride on tram No 6. There are also limited international services to the other cities.
- **Trains from Venice, Vienna, Budapest** and other destinations arrive at the railway station in Zagreb. Central Zagreb is a 10-minute walk away or a short ride on tram No 6 or 13.

## Arriving by Sea

Car and passenger ferries from Italy arrive at the ports of Zadar, Split and Dubrovnik. In summer, there are extra services to the more popular islands and also to Pula and Rovinj in Istria. All of these ports are within walking distance of the city centre, except Dubrovnik. From Gruž harbour in Dubrovnik, buses 1A and 1B run frequently to the main bus station and to Pile Gate.

## Tourist Information Offices

There are tourist offices in all the main towns, cities and coastal resorts. Most staff speak good English and German and can supply you with free local maps and additional information. You will also find private tourist agencies operating in most towns and these are usually the best places to find private accommodation and book local excursions. The biggest private tourist agency is Atlas (www.atlas-croatia.com), which has offices all over the country. The head tourist information office is in Dubrovnik (tel: 020 442 222).

**Zagreb**: Trg Bana Jelačića 11; 01 4814 051; www.zagreb-touristinfo.hr; open Mon–Fri 8:30am–8pm, Sat 9am–5pm, Sun 10am–2pm
**Dubrovnik, Grad-1**: Široka 1; 020 323 587; www.tzdubrovnik.hr; open Mon–Sat 9am–7pm, Sun 9am–2pm
**Dubrovnik, Pile:** Dubrovačkih branitelja 7; 020 427 591, 020 426 253; open Mon–Fri 9am–4pm, Sat 9am–2pm, closed Sun
**Dubrovnik, Grad-2:** Od sv. Dominika 7; 020 323 887, 020 323 889; open Mon–Fri 8am–4pm, Sat 9am–1pm, closed Sun
**Dubrovnik, Gruž:** Obala S. Radića 27; 020 417 983; open Mon–Fri 9am–4pm, Sat 9am–2pm, closed Sun
**Split**: Peristil; 021 345 606; www.visitsplit.com
**Pula**: Forum 3; 052 212 987; www.pulainfo.hr

---

### Admission Charges
The cost of admission for museums and places of interest featured in this guide is indicated by the following price categories.
**€** under 20kn      **€€** 20kn–40kn      **€€€** over 40kn

# Getting Around

## Driving in Croatia

- Drivers **bringing their own cars** into Croatia will need to show a driving licence, insurance certificate and registration documents.
- **Car rental** is available at airports and in all the main towns and resorts. You must be over 21 and have a passport, driving licence and credit card.
- The **best deals** are usually found in advance by booking online through one of the major international chains (see below). If you need a car for a few days only, local companies offer competitive rates, though you should check carefully the levels of insurance cover and excess.
- Keep your passport, driving licence and car rental documents **with you at all times**, and never leave them unattended in the car.

## Car Rental Agencies

**Budget**: 01 4805 688; www.budget.hr (Zagreb only)
**Europcar**: 01 6265 008; www.europcar.hr (Zagreb airport only)
**Hertz**: 01 4846 777; www.hertz.hr (Zagreb only)
**Holiday Autos**: www.holidayautos.com
**National**: 021 399 043; www.nationalcar.hr
**Sixt**: 01 6651 599; www.sixt.hr

## Driving Essentials

- Drive on the right.
- **Seat belts** are compulsory for the driver and all passengers.
- **Children under 12** must sit in the back of the car.
- The use of **mobile phones** while driving is forbidden.
- **Headlights** must be on at all times.
- **Speed limits** are 50kph (31mph) in urban areas, 80kph (49mph) on minor roads, 110kph (68mph) on main roads and 130kph (80mph) on toll motorways. The maximum speed for vehicles towing caravans is 80kph (49mph).
- A strict **drink-driving law** introduced in 2004 has reduced the blood-alcohol limit to zero. It is now illegal to drive after even moderate consumption of alcohol.
- In the case of an **accident**, you must call the police on 92.
- **Breakdown assistance** is available from Hrvatski Autoklub by calling 987.

## Roads and Tolls

- The **A3 motorway** runs west from Zagreb to the Slovenian border and east to Lipovac on the border with Serbia. This is the Croatian section of the *autocesta*, the major route across the former Yugoslavia, linking the capitals of Slovenia, Croatia and Serbia.
- **Other motorways** connect Zagreb with Rijeka, Krapina and Goričan on the Hungarian border. There is also a Y-shaped network of motorways throughout Istria, linking Rijeka with Pazin, Pula and Slovenia and eventually joining up with the Italian motorway system.
- All motorways are **subject to tolls**. In most cases you collect a ticket when you enter and pay on exit. Payment can be made in Croatian kuna, euros or by credit card. Typical toll fees for a standard car are 26kn from Zagreb to Varaždin, 56kn from Zagreb to Rijeka and 157kn from Zagreb to Split.
- The most **scenic drive** in Croatia is the Magistrala highway, which follows the coastline for 600km (372 miles) from Rijeka to Dubrovnik. Although this is a spectacular drive, the road is single-carriageway for most of its length and gets clogged up with holiday traffic in summer.

- The **A1 motorway** from Zagreb to Split will be extended to Dubrovnik by 2012, cutting several hours off journey times. The distance from Zagreb to Split is 380km (236 miles).
- **Tolls are also charged** for the Učka tunnel linking Rijeka to Istria, the Mirna bridge between Poreč and Novigrad and the road bridge to Krk.

---

**Driving Through Bosnia**
Check your insurance carefully if you plan to take a rental car into neighbouring countries, particularly Bosnia-Hercegovina, Serbia and Montenegro. An exception can be made for the area around Neum, a 9km (5.5-mile) corridor of Bosnia-Hercegovina on the Magistrala highway between Split and Dubrovnik.

---

## Buses and Trains

- **Buses connect main towns and cities** to outlying villages and coastal resorts.
- **Services range from** luxury air-conditioned inter-city coaches to local buses on the Adriatic islands.
- **Bus fares from the mainland** to the islands, such as Dubrovnik to Korčula or Rijeka to Rab, usually include the cost of the ferry.
- For **timetables and bookings**, ask at the nearest bus station.
- The **railway network** covers most major cities, with the exception of Dubrovnik.
- **Most rail lines** are concentrated in the north and east of the country, making this an efficient way to get around inland Croatia but less useful on the coast.
- **Rail travel is generally slower than buses, but high-speed trains now make the journey from Zagreb to Split in just over five hours.**
- **For detailed timetables**, contact the main railway station in Zagreb (tel: 060 333 444) or see the Croatian Railways website (www.hznet.hr).

## City Transport in Zagreb

- Zagreb has an **efficient network** of local buses and trams operated by ZET (www.zet.hr).
- The **main tram hubs** are the railway station, bus station and Trg Bana Jelačića.
- **Maps** are displayed at all tram stops.
- **Tickets** (8kn) can be bought from ZET kiosks near the terminals and news kiosks in Trg Bana Jelačića. They are slightly more expensive (10kn) if bought from the driver.
- **Tickets are validated** by punching them in the machine behind the driver.
- There are heavy fines (150kn) for travelling without a ticket.
- If you are spending a few days in Zagreb, it is worth getting hold of a **Zagreb Card**, valid for 24 hours (60kn) or 72 hours (90kn). It gives free access to all public transport, including the funicular to Gradec and the bus to Medvednica, as well as discounts at museums.

## City Transport in Dubrovnik

- Buses in Dubrovnik are **operated by Libertas** (www.libertasdubrovnik.hr).
- The **most useful routes** are those connecting the hotels on the Lapad peninsula with the old town.
- Tickets (8kn) can be bought from **news kiosks and Libertas counters** outside the Pile Gate. They are slightly more expensive if bought from the drivers, who do not give change, so you must pay the exact fare, 10kn.
- Tickets are **validated by punching them** in the machine behind the driver.

## Taxis

- Taxis are available in **all main towns**, cities and resorts.
- **Fares are metered**; you usually pay a flat fare of around 25kn plus an extra amount per kilometre, with extra charges levied at night and on Sundays.

## Ferries

- The **Jadrolinija ferry company** operates car and passenger services between the mainland and the major islands.
- There is also a **daily car ferry** from Rijeka to Dubrovnik, calling at Zadar, Split, Stari Grad (Hvar), Korčula and Mljet.
- **A full list of routes, fares and timetables** is available from Jadrolinija offices and on the website (www.jadrolinija.hr).
- **Foot passengers** can simply arrive at the harbour and buy tickets from the quayside kiosk.
- **Car passengers** must join a queue, which is often lengthy in summer, so at peak times it is best to arrive at least two hours before departure.
- **Prior reservations** are not possible on local ferries.
- Tickets and cabins for the **main Rijeka to Dubrovnik coastal route** can be booked in advance.
- Between June and September, there are **additional fast catamaran services** linking the islands to the mainland.
- **Catamarans** run throughout the year to the islands of Mljet, Korčula, Hvar, Vis and Lastovo; these are quicker than conventional ferries, but also more expensive and the disadvantage is that you cannot go on deck. Cars are not allowed on these services.
- The timetable is often geared to getting the **islanders to the mainland** for work, so there may only be one boat per day in each direction.

### Jadrolinija Offices
**Dubrovnik**: 020 418 000
**Split**: 021 338 333
**Rijeka**: 051 211 444

# Accommodation

Croatia has a range of accommodation to suit all budgets and tastes, from large seaside hotels to rooms in private houses. In summer most hotel rooms are pre-booked by tour operators and package-tourists, but it is almost always possible to find private accommodation by asking around in local agencies or looking for signs advertising *sobe* (rooms) to rent. Some of the best examples of places to stay are listed at the end of the regional chapters.

## Hotels

- The majority of hotels were built during the tourist boom between the 1960s and 1980s. These tend to be **large, modern and well equipped**, though lacking in atmosphere and architectural style. Many have been upgraded since the 1991–5 war, when they were converted to house refugees. Most have swimming pools and a wide range of sports and leisure facilities, restaurants and nightclubs.
- **Most hotels on the coast and islands** operate from April to October, while hotels in Zagreb and inland are open all year. Book ahead during the peak months of June, July and August.

- A recent trend has been the opening of **small, family-run and boutique hotels** in the middle of historic towns. Many of these are members of the Association of Small and Family Hotels (tel: 021 317 880; www.omh.hr).

## Private Accommodation

- The **cheapest rooms on the islands and coast** are often in private accommodation. These range from comfortable apartments with a kitchen, bathroom and balcony, to a spare bedroom with shared bathroom in a family home.
- In **busy tourist towns**, you will be met at the bus station or ferry port by landladies offering rooms or holding up signs saying *sobe* (rooms) or *apartmani* (apartments).
- You can **reserve private rooms** through one of the travel agencies found in all main towns and resorts. This will usually work out a little more expensive, but the accommodation is registered and of a guaranteed standard.
- There are **surcharges for tourist tax** and for stays of less than three days.

## Agrotourism

- One of the biggest growth areas has been in **rural farmstays** or agrotourism (▶ 16–18), which has taken off particularly in Istria and inland areas such as the Zagorje.
- **Rural accommodation** is usually indicated by signs advertising *agroturizam* or *seoski turizam*.

## Camping

- Croatia has **over 150 official campsites**, equipped with hot water, showers and toilets. Many have restaurants and sports facilities, including swimming pools.
- The majority are on the coast and islands, while a few are inland beside rivers and lakes. Be aware that some of these campsites are **reserved for naturists**.
- Most campsites are **open from May to September**.
- **A full list of campsites** is found at www.croatia.hr and www.camping.hr.

## Off the Beaten Track

- A number of **lighthouses** have been converted into unusual self-catering accommodation (▶ 18).
- **Travel agencies in Murter** rent out old stone cottages on the Kornati islands for a 'Robinson Crusoe' experience. There is no electricity or running water and all the cooking is done by gas. Water comes from a well and supplies are delivered by boat twice a week.
  Contact Kornatturist (tel: 022 435 854; www.kornatturist.hr) or Lori (tel: 022 435 631; www.touristagency-lori.hr).

---

### Accommodation Prices

The symbols refer to the approximate cost per person per night of a double room in summer. Prices drop considerably outside the peak season. Half-board accommodation, which is included in the price of most package holidays, is often only marginally more expensive than bed-and-breakfast. Hotels also levy a tourist tax, which varies according to season.

€ under 250kn          €€ 250kn–500kn          €€€ over 500kn

# Food and Drink

Croatian cuisine is a fascinating blend of Mediterranean, Balkan and Central European influences. Regional cuisines reflect the country's history and geography, with light, fresh, Italian-style cooking dominating on the coast and heavier, spicier fare served in the inland and highland regions.

## Eating Out – A Practical Guide

- Most restaurants serve both **Croatian and international dishes**.
- A *konoba* or *gostionica* is a **rustic-style tavern** specializing in more authentic Croatian cuisine.
- **Mealtimes are around** noon–3 for lunch and 7–10 for supper, though most places stay open throughout the day from 9am–11pm.
- Reservations are rarely necessary, except at the **smartest establishments**.
- Most places make a **small cover charge** for bread.
- It is customary to **leave a tip** of around 10 per cent.

## What to Eat

- **Starters** include *pršut* (cured ham) and *sir* (cheese).
- **Pasta dishes and risottos** are listed as 'warm starters', but are usually enough for a main course.
- **Fresh fish and seafood** predominate on the coast. Fish (*riba*) is usually plain grilled and sold by weight. Other popular dishes are seafood risotto, octopus salad, shrimps *buzara* (with garlic and white wine) and *brudet* (Dalmatian fish stew).
- **Dalmatian meat dishes** include *pastičada* (beef stewed with sweet wine), *janjetina* (spit-roast lamb) and veal or lamb cooked under a *peka* (metal bell) placed in the embers of a fire.
- **Istrian cooking** is heavily influenced by Italy, featuring *njoki* (gnocchi), *fuži* (pasta) and truffles.
- **Steaks and schnitzels** are popular everywhere, but especially in the inland regions. In Zagreb, look out for *zagrebački odrezak*, a breaded schnitzel stuffed with ham and cheese.
- **Inland and mountain cuisine** is similar to that of central Europe, with dishes such as *gulaš* (goulash) and *grah* (bean stew).
- **Slavonian cooking** is particularly spicy, featuring *kulen* (salami) and *fiš paprikaš* (fish stew).
- The **national snack** is *ćevapčići*, grilled meatballs served with raw onions, *ajvar* (spicy aubergine and pepper relish) and bread or chips.
- **Side dishes** include chips, boiled potatoes, rice, pasta, salads and *blitva*, which is similar to spinach and is either steamed or fried with potatoes, garlic and olive oil.
- *Pekarnica* (bakeries) sell a wide range of **breads**, as well as *burek* (filo pastry stuffed with minced meat or cheese).
- **Desserts** include *palačinke* (pancakes) with walnuts, chocolate or jam. A *slastičarnica* is a pastry-shop; most also sell delicious ice-cream.

## What to Drink

- Croatia produces an **excellent variety of wines**. Cheaper local wines are sold by the litre, whereas more expensive wines are sold by the bottle.
- **Red wines** to look out for include Dingač, Postup and Plavac Mali from the Pelješac peninsula, and Teran from Istria.
- **White wines** include Malvazija from Istria, Graševina from Slavonia, Grk and Pošip from Korčula and Vugava from Vis,
- Prošek is a **sweet red wine** from Dalmatia, an apéritif or dessert wine.

- **Mixed drinks** include *bevanda* (wine and water), *gemišt* (white wine spritzer), *bambus* (red wine and cola) and *miš-maš* (red wine and Fanta).
- The best brands of **lager** are *Karlovačko* and *Ožujsko*. Tomislav is a dark beer from Zagreb.
- Fierce **grappa-like spirits** are drunk both before and after the meal, and are sometimes offered on the house by waiters. They include *šlijvovica* (plum brandy), *travarica* (herb brandy) and *biska* (mistletoe brandy from Istria). A sweeter alternative is *orahovac* (walnut liqueur).
- *Mineralna voda* (mineral water) can be either *gazirana* (sparkling) or *negazirana* (still).
- Bars sell a range of **fruit juices**, as well as many international brands of soft drinks.
- **Coffee** is usually espresso or cappuccino, though some restaurants serve Turkish coffee, traditionally drunk at home by Croatians.

---

### Food Prices
The symbols refer to the approximate prices for a starter, main course, salad and house wine or water.

€ under 100kn       €€ 100kn–200kn       €€€ over 200kn

---

# Shopping

Croatia has come a long way since the days of state communism, when bland department stores and supermarkets were notable mainly for their empty shelves. Consumerism is no longer a dirty word and the big cities have boutiques and fashion stores to rival neighbouring Italy. Zagreb is the undisputed shopping capital of Croatia, though you will also find a good range of shops in Split and Dubrovnik.

## Practicalities
- Most shops are open Monday to Friday 8–8, and Saturday 9–2, although some **close in the middle of the day**, opening from around 9–1 and 5–8. In larger towns and coastal resorts in season, many stay open on Sundays.
- **Markets** are generally open Monday to Saturday from 8–2, though a few open on Sundays as well.
- The monthly **agricultural fairs** in the towns of inland Istria, such as Buzet, Motovun, Pazin and Vodnjan, have traditional local foods, hand-made goods, folk music and dancing. Ask at the local tourist offices for further information.
- **Credit cards** are accepted in an increasing number of shops.

## What to Buy
- **Popular souvenirs** include lace from Pag, lavender products from Hvar, jewellery from Dubrovnik and gingerbread hearts from around Zagreb.
- **Artists sell their work** in the street at many coastal towns in summer. Some of the best places to buy contemporary art are Rovinj, Grožnjan, Dubrovnik and Hlebine.
- A **Croata silk tie** (► 63) makes an unusual present.
- Croatian **wines, spirits, truffles and olive oil** all make good souvenirs.
- Farmers at local markets sell a variety of **home-made spirits and liqueurs** in attractive bottles.

# Entertainment

From top-class music and drama to traditional festivals, sports and outdoor activities, there is always something to do in Croatia. More details can be found from tourist offices and in each of the regional chapters of this book.

## Music and Drama

- The top venue is the **Croatian National Theatre** in Zagreb (➤ 64), home to the National Ballet and National Opera. More than 200 performances of drama, ballet and opera are held here each year between September and July. There are also branches of the Croatian National Theatre in Osijek, Rijeka, Split and Varaždin.

- Almost every town along the coast holds a **cultural festival** in summer, with a series of open-air performances under the name of 'Musical Evenings' or 'Summer Nights'.

- The **big events** in Croatia are the summer festivals in Dubrovnik (➤ 162) and Split (➤ 140), with drama, opera and concerts in the streets of the old town.

- Another spectacular concert venue is the magnificent **Roman arena in Pula** (➤ 112).

## Folklore and Festivals

- Croatia has a **rich folk music tradition**, from the *klapa* male voice choirs of Dalmatia to the *kolo* dances and *tamburica* (mandolin) music of Slavonia. Many hotels lay on folklore shows for their guests, but for something more authentic, try the International Folklore Festival in Zagreb in July or the folk festivals at Slavonski Brod and Đakovo (➤ 88).

- The *moreška* **sword dance** (➤ 26–27) can be seen on Korčula throughout the summer and at the Festival of Sword Dances in July and August.

- Most towns and villages have their own feast day, when the **patron saint's festival** is marked by a religious procession through the streets, fireworks and dancing.

- The **pre-Lenten Carnival** is also celebrated across the country; the biggest parades are in Rijeka (➤ 105), Samobor (➤ 82) and Lastovo (➤ 155).

## Sport and Outdoor Activities

- Croatians are passionate about **football** (➤ 30) and there is huge rivalry between the two biggest teams, Dinamo Zagreb and Hajduk Split. The season lasts from August to May with a two-month winter break between December and February. Most matches are played at weekends and it is usually possible to get tickets.

- Croatia's **biggest tennis event** is the ATP Croatia Open, held at Umag in late July.

- **Swimming** is popular at beaches along the Adriatic coast. There are few sandy beaches, but many resorts have concrete sunbathing platforms with steps into the sea.

- Walking, bicycling, climbing, horseback-riding, canoeing, kayaking and rafting are all possible in Croatia's mountains and rivers, **together with adventure sports** such as paragliding and canyoning.

- On the coast, numerous operators offer **scuba diving excursions**, while windsurfing is possible at Bol on Brač and Viganj on the Pelješac peninsula. Another option is to charter a yacht to explore the Kornati Islands (➤ 134).

# Zagreb

# Getting Your Bearings

Zagreb, with around a million inhabitants, one in four of the country's population, is easily Croatia's biggest city. This is the political, economic and cultural heart of the nation, which makes it easy to forget that it has only been a state capital since 1991. For most of its history, Zagreb has lived in the shadow of Vienna, as a provincial outpost of the Austro-Hungarian empire, or of the former Yugoslav capital Belgrade. Only in the last few years has it rediscovered its confidence as a youthful, vibrant, forward-looking city.

Groblje Mirogoj **12**
Medvednica **11**

Muzej
Grada Zagreba **4**

Fondacija
Ivan Meštrović **3**
Prirodoslovni
Muzej

KAPTOL

Sv
Marka    Sabor
Hrvatski Muzej         Kamenita
Naivne Umjetnosti **5**   Vrata    Gornji **2** Grad

Trg A
Stepinca

Kula            Sv
Lotrščak        Katerina    Dolac    Katedrala    Maksimirski **10**
                                                   Perivoj

Britanski
trg      ILICA         ILICA    Trg Bana **1**
ILICA                           Jelačića                      J Iblerov
                                                              trg
         Trg Petra                 JURIŠIĆEVA               MARTIČEV
         Preradovića   Bogovićeva   PRAŠKA

                              N TESLE    AMRUŠEVA
                                        Arheološki **9**
PRILAZ GYURE DEŽELIĆA                   Muzej
           Trg Maršala
Muzej Za   Tita                 Trg Nikole
Umjetnost i Obrt **6**          Šubića
           Hrvatsko             Zrinjskog    R BOŠKOVIĆA
KLAIĆEVA   Narodno Kazalište                 Strossmayerova
           A. HEBRANGA                        Galerija Starih
Muzej     Rooseveltov   Etnografski Muzej **8**  Majstora
Mimara **7**  trg                             Strossm
KRŠRJAGOVA     Mažuranićev   DONJI GRAD       trg     P HATZA
               trg
               J ŽERJAVIĆA    BARUNA TRENKA
                              Zagrebačko
           Marulićev         Kazalište
           trg               Lutaka    Trg kralja       A Šenoina
                                       Tomislava
           VODNIKOVA         MIHANOVIĆEVA
                                         ŽELJEZNIČKA    KNEZA BRANIMIRA
                                         STANICA
Tehnički            Botanički
Muzej               vrt

0              500 metres
0              500 yards

## ★ Don't Miss

## At Your Leisure

Zagreb lies between the wooded slopes of Medvednica to the north and the River Sava to the south. It consisted originally of two fortified hilltop settlements – the religious base of Kaptol, still dominated by its cathedral, and the rival political capital of Gradec. Between them, these two make up the area known as Gornji Grad (Upper Town). In the 19th century, the city expanded and the Donji Grad (Lower Town) was developed, with wide boulevards, museums and grand Austro-Hungarian buildings linked by a green 'horseshoe' of parks, promenades and squares. Much of this district was built following an earthquake in 1880, giving the city a unified, central European feel.

The two halves of town meet at Trg Bana Jelačića, Zagreb's central square. With its popular café terraces and hordes of commuters catching trams, the square is busy from morning to night and makes a natural starting point for any visit to the city.

Page 41:
Escape from
the city to
Zagreb's
relaxing
botanical
gardens

Right: The
Croatian flag
flies outside
the parliament
complex, in
Zagreb

# In Two Days

If you're not quite sure where to begin your travels, this itinerary recommends a practical and enjoyable two-day tour of Zagreb, taking in some of the best places to see using the Getting Your Bearings map on the previous page. Spend one day exploring the old town and the other out in the suburbs as you discover the many different faces of Zagreb.

## Day 1

### Morning

Start with coffee and pastries on ❶ **Trg Bana Jelačića** (➤ 46–48), an essential Zagreb experience and the best place to sample the pulse of the city. While you're here, visit the tourist office on the corner of the square to pick up a map and a Zagreb Card (➤ 48). After coffee, climb the steps to Dolac market (➤ 63), at its liveliest on weekday mornings.

### Lunch

Take the funicular (left) up to ❷ **Gornji Grad** (➤ 49–51), arriving in time to see the cannon being fired from the Kula Lotrščak (Lotrščak Tower) at noon. Have lunch beneath the tower at Pod Gričkim Topom (➤ 62) whose terrace offers wonderful views.

### Afternoon

Take your time strolling around Gradec, with its churches, palaces and cobbled streets. There are several good museums here, but if you have time for only one, make it the ❸ **Fondacija Ivan Meštrović** (➤ 52–53), dedicated to the work of Croatia's greatest modern sculptor. Leave Gradec through the Kamenita Vrata (Stone Gate) and wander back down to Trg Bana Jelačića, pausing to visit the cathedral on the way.

## Evening

The streets around Trg Bana Jelačića (below left) are at their best during the early evening *korzo*, when people dress up and promenade through the town. Stop for a beer or an ice-cream at one of the outdoor cafés on Bogovićeva before going for dinner at nearby Boban (► 61).

# Day 2

## Morning

Time to explore Donji Grad (Lower Town). Begin outside the railway station by the equestrian statue of King Tomislav and follow a series of park squares northwards until you reach Trg Nikole Šubića Zrinskog (Zrinjevac), with its bandstand, fountain and statues. On one side of the square is the **9 Arheološki Muzej** (► 58) – after a quick look around, you can grab a drink at the Lapidarium, a courtyard café surrounded by Roman sculpture.

## Afternoon

Do what the locals do and escape the city for a few hours. The easy option is to hop on tram 11 or 12 from Trg Bana Jelačića for a picnic in **10 Maksimirski Perivoj** (► 58). Alternatively, take bus No 106 from outside the cathedral to **12 Groblje Mirogoj** (► 59), then walk down the hill and pick up the tram to **11 Medvednica** (► 59). Check with the tourist office whether a cable car is back in operation, or buses from Mihaljevac will whisk you up the mountain; if you have the energy, you can walk back through the woods before returning to Trg Bana Jelačića by tram.

## Evening

Ask at the tourist office for a copy of their monthly leaflet of concert and theatre listings. If you can, take in a show at the Hrvatsko Narodno Kazalište (Croatian National Theatre, above), a sumptuous opera house which opened in 1895 (► 64).

# ❶ Trg Bana Jelačića

This broad paved square, where the old town meets the new,
is the symbolic heart of Zagreb. Café life rules here, with
everyone from the president downwards meeting on the
café terraces on weekend mornings to read the newspapers,
talk politics, sport and gossip. Cars are not allowed in the
square, but trams trundle to and fro, bringing commuters and
shoppers from the outlying suburbs. With newspaper kiosks
and flower stalls against a backdrop of imposing 19th-century
Habsburg architecture, Trg Bana Jelačića central square
presents a lively scene.

It was laid out as the city's main square in 1850, but its
present character dates from 1866, when the **equestrian
statue** of Governor Josip Jelačić (1801–59) was placed here,
seven years after his death. This popular figure was appointed
to quell anti-Hungarian feeling and the statue recalls his
triumphant entry into Zagreb in 1848. Despite being a
servant of the Austro-Hungarian empire, he became an ardent
Croatian nationalist; he abolished feudalism, waged war on
Hungary and united Croatia, Slavonia and Dalmatia into a
single state.

**Trg Bana
Jelačića
is a hive
of activity,
watched over
by the statue
of Governor
Jelačića on
horseback**

    The statue has witnessed changing fortunes over the years.
In 1947, after the Communists took power, it was dismantled
and replaced with a monument to socialist women, while the
square was renamed Trg Republike (Republic Square). The

**Fuit and vegetable stalls in the atmospheric Dolac market, Zagreb**

statue was never destroyed, but kept in a cellar by a museum curator, ready for its eventual restoration. Finally, in 1990, as Croatia prepared for independence, this symbol of Croatian nationalism was returned to its original setting, only this time the governor's sword pointed not to the old enemy in Budapest but to the new one in Belgrade. Later, the sword was moved again, pointing directly southwards to the Serbian-held capital at Knin during the war against the Republic of the Serbian Krajina in the 1990s.

These days, tourists pose for photos beside the statue and locals arrange to meet beneath the nearby clock. This is a good place to start the *korzo*, the **nightly promenade** that is as much a part of Zagreb ritual as the *volta* in Athens or the *passeggiata* in Rome. Fashionably dressed teenagers, students and office workers appear magically at the same time each evening to walk, talk and flirt, and above all to see and be seen. Most of the action takes place in the pedestrianized streets to the south of Trg Bana Jelačića, especially Bogovićeva and Gajeva, with their many bars and ice-cream parlours.

## The Market

All around Trg Bana Jelačića are elegant examples of Vienna Secession architecture, a late 19th-century Austro-Hungarian movement broadly equivalent to art nouveau. A passage on the north side of the square leads to **Dolac**, the city's main market since 1930. Croatians are passionate about the quality of their fresh produce and there is nowhere better to see the range of goods available. An indoor market hall contains stalls selling bread, pasta, cheese, hams and sausages, nuts, grains, and olives, while an annexe on the western side is devoted to fish. Upstairs, farmers from the surrounding countryside sell fruit, vegetables, eggs and herbs. The market is open daily from 8am, arrive early if you want to soak up the atmosphere.

### TAKING A BREAK

Take your pick from the various cafés on the edge of Trg Bana
Jelačića square. **Mala Kavana**, on the north side close to the
equestrian statue, is a popular choice in a prime people-
watching spot. Other good options are **Ban Café**, on the same
side; **Gradska Kavana**, on the northeast corner closest to the
cathedral; and **Dubrovnik Kavana**, on the south side of the
square. If you want something more substantial, there are
several inexpensive grill restaurants on the lower terrace of the
Dolac market. Rubelj (▶ 62) has outside seating with large
parasols, a number of basic dishes to choose from and is a
popular choice for lunch.

Trg Bana
Jelačića is a
great place
for people-
watching

➕ 201 D3   🚋 Tram 1, 6, 11, 12, 13, 14, 17

**Tourist Information Office**
✉ Trg Bana Jelačića 11   ☎ 01 4814 051
🕓 Mon–Fri 8:30–8, Sat 9–5, Sun 10–2

## TRG BANA JELAČIĆA: INSIDE INFO

**Top tips** The tourist information office, in the southeast corner of the
square, sells the **Zagreb Card**, which is well worth buying if you plan to spend
a few days in the city. Valid for 72 hours, it gives unlimited use of all public
transport in Zagreb (including the funicular to Gradec and the Medvednica
cable car) and half-price entry to museums, as well as discounts at
restaurants, shops, theatres and car rental agencies.

■ Ilica, which runs west from Trg Bana Jelačića, is Zagreb's **principal shopping
street**. Just off the square, the Vincek *slastičarnica* (pastry shop) at Ilica 18
sells some of the most delicious ice-cream sundaes in town.

# ❷ Gornji Grad

The medieval district of Gornji Grad (Upper Town), with its cobbled streets, churches and red-tiled roofs, is the most atmospheric part of the city. It was built on a hill at the end of the 11th century and is the original nucleus of Zagreb, though little remains from that period; most of what you see today was built after 1880, when an earthquake destroyed much of the old town.

Gornji Grad consists of two separate settlements, divided by the dried-up riverbed of what is now Tkalčićeva. To the west is **Gradec**, the focus of government since the 17th century; to the east is **Kaptol**, the ecclesiastical capital, with its cathedral, archbishop's palace and religious institutions.

The most enjoyable way of reaching the upper town is on the **funicular tramway** (*uspinjača*), which takes less than a minute to make the ascent from Tomićeva. Take a seat at the lower end of the carriage to enjoy the views over Donji Grad as you climb. The funicular has been operating since 1893 and has become a much-loved feature of Zagreb. It departs every 10 minutes between 6:30am and midnight, so you shouldn't have long to wait.

*The Lotrščak tower in Gornji Grad*

## Gradec

**Kula Lotrščak** (Burglars' Tower), opposite the upper funicular terminus, is the only surviving part of Gradec's 13th-century fortifications. It is named after the bell called *campana latrunculorum*, the 'bell of thieves', which once chimed each night before the closing of the city gates. The tower was rebuilt in the mid-19th century, with a spiral staircase leading to an observation gallery; since that time it has been used as a warehouse, wine cellar, café and billiards club. Those of a nervous disposition should keep away at midday, when a cannon is fired from the tower. It was first used on New Year's Day 1877 as a signal for the city's bellringers, and the citizens of Zagreb soon learned to set their watches by the sound of the Grič cannon. One man, Marijan Fröbe, acted as cannoneer for 45 years from 1928 to 1973; since 1975 the cannoneer has been a man called Stjepan Možar.

A short distance from here, **Trg Svetog Marka** (St Mark's Square) is the focal point of Gradec. At its heart is **St Mark's Church**, the oldest parish church in Zagreb. The church is notable for its mosaic roof tiles, which date from 1882 and feature the historic coats of arms of Croatia (the red and white chequerboard, still used in the national flag), Dalmatia (three lions), Slavonia (a pine marten running between the rivers Sava and Drava) and Zagreb (a castle). Inside the church you will find a number of sculptures by Ivan Meštrović, including a Crucifixion and a Madonna with Child. On either side of the square stand the most powerful political institutions in Croatia – the **Sabor** (Croatian parliament), where independence from Yugoslavia was declared in 1991, and the **Banski Dvori** (Governor's Palace), which now houses the offices of the presidency.

From the east side of St Mark's Square, Ulica Kamenita leads to the

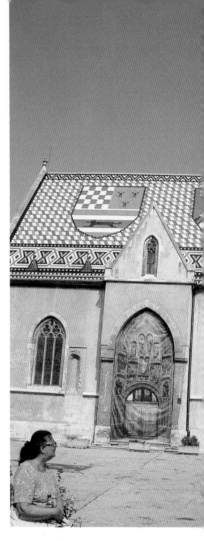

St Mark's Church with its colourfully tiled roof is a focal point of Gradec

**Kamenita Vrata** (Stone Gate), which dates from the 13th century and is the only survivor of the four original entrances to Gradec. When a fire in 1731 destroyed most of the nearby houses, an image of the Virgin Mary was found in the ashes and a chapel was built to house it inside the restored gate. In recent years, this has become an important place of pilgrimage. Nuns sell votive candles from a small shop alongside the shrine and the air is thick with incense and dripping wax.

## Kaptol

From here it is a short walk to Kaptol, dominated by the neo-Gothic twin spires of its **cathedral**. The first church dates from around 1102, but was later destroyed and rebuilt in Gothic style. Following the earthquake of 1880, the cathedral had to be rebuilt yet again, by the German architect Hermann Bollé.

The biggest draw seems to be the **sarcophagus of Cardinal Alojzije Stepinac** (1898–1960), a former archbishop of Zagreb who was accused of collaborating with the fascist Ustaše regime and was subsequently jailed and placed under house arrest by Tito. Since independence in 1991, he has become a Croatian nationalist hero and was beatified by the Pope on a visit to Croatia in 1998. His tomb is usually surrounded by visitors paying their respects; note also the relief by Ivan Meštrović in the north wall, showing Stepinac kneeling before Christ. Behind here, in the sacristy, are some 13th-century frescoes.

The column outside the cathedral is topped by a gilded statue of the Virgin surrounded by angels, the work of the Viennese sculptor Anton Fernkorn (1813–78), who also designed the statue of Governor Jelačić in Trg Bana Jelačića.

## TAKING A BREAK

The cafés on Katarinin Trg, near the Lotršcak Tower, make good places for a relaxing open-air drink. For lunch, dine al fresco in the garden or on the terrace of **Pod Gričkim Topom** (➤ 62), or feast on traditional Croatian dishes at **Stara Vura** (tel: 01 4851 368; closed Sun), in the cellar of the Muzej Grada Zagreba.

___

**Kula Lotršcak**
✚ 200 C3  ✉ Strossmayerovo Šetalište 9
☎ 01 4851 768  🕐 May–Oct Tue–Sun 11–8
💷 Inexpensive

**Katedrala (cathedral)**
✚ 201 D3  ✉ Kaptol 31  ☎ 01 4814 727
🕐 Daily 10–6  💷 Free

___

## GORNJI GRAD: INSIDE INFO

**Top tip** Take a stroll along **Strossmayerovo Šetalište**, a promenade that follows the line of the old city walls, with benches, shady walkways and views across the rooftops of Donji Grad to the tower blocks of Novi Zagreb, beyond the River Sava in the distance.

**Hidden gem** Children will enjoy the **Prirodoslovni Muzej**, a natural history museum housed in an old theatre at Ulica Demetrova 1 (open Tue, Wed, Fri 10–5, Thu 10–10, Sat 10–7, Sun 10–1), with an impressive collection of stuffed animals displayed in old-fashioned cabinets.

# ❸ Fondacija Ivan Meštrović

This engaging and intimate museum provides an excellent introduction to the work of Ivan Meštrović (1883–1962), one of the best-known sculptors of the 20th century and one of the few Croatians to have become famous beyond his country's borders. Spend any amount of time in Croatia and you will soon become familiar with his work, which can be seen in churches, parks and plazas from Zagreb to Split.

Meštrović was born in Slavonia to a family of itinerant agricultural workers. Despite a lack of formal education – he had to teach himself to read and write – his artistic ability was soon spotted and at the age of 15 he was apprenticed to a stonemason in Split. Later he studied in Vienna and worked in Paris and Rome, where he made contact with the French sculptor Auguste Rodin (1840–1917). By 1905 he had produced *Well of Life*, a group of bronze figures around a fountain, which are now on display outside the Croatian National Theatre.

**HIGHLIGHTS**

■ *Woman in Agony* (1928): this contorted nude figure, sculpted in bronze, stands in the middle of the atrium, a small courtyard entered from the street before going into the museum.

■ *History of the Croats* (1932): this bronze sculpture in the garden of the musum is full of political symbolism, featuring a mother as the emblem of the nation holding a stone tablet inscribed in Glagolitic script (▶ 173) on her lap.

■ *Mother and Child* (1942): on display in the artist's studio, this beautiful, unfinished walnut carving shows the tender features of a mother embracing her child.

■ *Olga Meštrović feeding Tvrtko* (1925): is an intimate portrait of Meštrović's second wife breastfeeding their young son and it has a Madonna-like quality.

After two decades abroad, Meštrović returned to Croatia and settled in this 17th-century house in Zagreb, where he lived and worked from 1924 to 1942. As an active campaigner for Croat-Serb unity, he was imprisoned by the fascist Ustaše government and spent his later life in exile in the United States.

With much of the artist's furniture on display, the house retains the atmosphere of a family home. The main attraction, however, is the collection of over 100 of his sculptures in wood, bronze and stone, representing some 40 years of his work and providing a good overview of his style, which combined elements of classical sculpture and folk art. The most common themes are religious imagery and female nudes, though there are also some touching portraits of his family.

**Left: Bust of Ivan Meštrovic (1883–1962)**

**Above: Bronz sculpture in the Fondacija Ivan Meštrović**

### TAKING A BREAK

**Lanterna** (Ulica Mletačka 11; tel: 01 4851 818), across the street, serves inexpensive Croatian meals.

✚ 200 C4   ✉ Ulica Mletačka 8   ☎ 01 4851 123   🕐 Tue–Fri 10–6, Sat–Sun 10–2   💰 Moderate

---

## FONDACIJA IVAN MEŠTROVIĆ: INSIDE INFO

**In more depth** Although the major works are exhibited in the ground-floor studio and garden, make time to explore the **second-floor galleries**. Among the items on display are some plaster reliefs of the artist's parents, children and first wife, designed for the family mausoleum in Otavice, near Split. The original bronze doors of the mausoleum were looted by Serbian troops during their occupation of Croatia in the 1990s, making these surviving copies all the more significant.

# At Your Leisure

**Muzej Grada in Zagreb is filled with interesting artifacts**

## 4 Muzej Grada Zagreba

You could easily spend a couple of hours in the absorbing **Museum of the City of Zagreb**, which uses maps, photographs, scale models and artefacts to explain the history of Zagreb from its foundation in 1094 to the present day. It is housed in the **17th-century Convent** of the Poor Clares, along with the medieval Popov Turen (Priests' Tower) and an adjacent granary and school.

From the street with its *trompe-l'oeil* painted windows, which only serve to emphasize the seclusion of the enclosed order of nuns that once lived here, you enter through the courtyard, most notable for the fine sundial on its facade.

A recent renovation has uncovered various archaeological remains in the basement, and a tour of the museum begins with a walk through a reconstructed metal-working factory from the 1st century BC. From here,

you leap forward 1,000 years for an enjoyable tour of Zagreb's history, arranged chronologically, but with certain galleries devoted to themes such as shopping, theatres and parks.

Among the objects to look out for are the oldest known coat of arms of Zagreb, carved in stone in 1499; the original 17th-century stone figures of Jesus, Mary, the apostles and the archangel Gabriel from the cathedral portal; a set of brightly painted 'targets' awarded as prizes in competitions organized by the Zagreb shooting club, the city's first civic society, established in 1796; and some charming reconstructed shopfronts from 19th-century Ilica.

There is a large collection of political and tourist posters from the 20th century, and the final exhibit features video footage of the Serbian attack on the presidential palace in 1991, together with broken crockery and furniture. If you are feeling hungry, the Stara Vura (Old Clock), a barrel-vaulted stone cellar set into the medieval defensive wall in the basement, serves good Croatian food.

✛ 200 C4 ☒ Ulica Opatička 20
☎ 01 4851 364 ◷ Tue, Wed, Fri 10–6, Thu 10–10, Sat 11–7, Sun 10–2 💷 Moderate

## 5 Hrvatski Muzej Naivne Umjetnosti

This small museum gives a good introduction to the **Croatian naïve art movement**. Originating in the 1930s when a group of villagers in Hlebine (► 83) began painting vivid scenes of rural life on glass, the two key figures in the movement were Ivan Generalić (1914–92) and Franjo Mraz (1910–81). Before long there was a whole group of artists known as the Hlebine School. These were self-taught, peasant painters who drew what they saw, and their early work reflected scenes of everyday rural life. In time, the movement developed and became known internationally; the later generation of naïve artists, while similar in style, used greater technical complexity and their work became influenced by surrealism and magical realism.

The museum features an overview of naive art from the 1930s onwards, with an emphasis on the Hlebine School, but also including artists from Dalmatia and abroad. The first room is devoted to Generalić; it is interesting to compare his *Self-Portrait* (1975) with the contemporary portrait of *Father Fishing* (1974) by his son Josip (1936–2004). Also, here are the first works of Croatian naïve sculpture, including wooden figures of Adam and Eve and *Mother and Child* by Petar Smajić (1910–85).

🚩 200 C3  ✉ Ulica Svetog ćirila i Metoda 3
☎ 01 4851 911  🕐 Tue–Fri 10–6, Sat–Sun 10–1  💰 Moderate

## 🟢 Muzej Za Umjetnost i Obrt

The wide-ranging **Arts and Crafts Museum** is housed in a late 19th-century building designed by Hermann Bollé (1845–1916), the architect of the cathedral and Mirogoj cemetery. It was founded immediately following the earthquake of 1880 to preserve traditional works of art and craft in the face of the new threat of mass production.

The museum's collections of painting, sculpture, clocks, musical instruments, furniture, silverware and graphic design offers a broad sweep through the arts and it is easy to get overwhelmed, but it is manageable if you concentrate on a few key themes.

The highlight of the first floor is the sacred art collection, with altarpieces from northern Croatian churches (note the 17th-century Madonna from the village of Remetinec) and a number of statues from Zagreb cathedral.

The second-floor galleries feature art nouveau, art deco and 20th-century art and design, showing how Croatian art has developed alongside the mainstream European trends.

🚩 200 B2  ✉ Trg Maršala Tita 10
☎ 01 4882 111  🕐 Tue, Wed, Fri, Sat 10–7, Thu 10–10, Sun 10–2  💰 Moderate

## 🟢 Muzej Mimara

Zagreb's biggest museum is based entirely on the **personal collection** of the Croatian businessman Ante Topić Mimara (1898–1987), who made his fortune abroad and spent it amassing art works which he donated to the nation shortly before his death. Although there is nothing remotely Croatian about any of the objects on display, it is still a fascinating collection;

**This impressive statue outside Muzej Za Umjetnost i Obrt depicts the story of George and the Dragon**

*The Bather* by Renoir, Muzej Mimara

Mimara's eclectic tastes encompassed everything from Egyptian glassware and Persian carpets to Russian icons, Chinese jade, old masters and the French Impressionists. You need to allow at least two hours to do it justice. Room 1 contains some of the oldest objects, including a Christian chalice from Alexandria dating from the 3rd century AD, acquired by Mimara at the age of 19 and said to have been the catalyst for his lifelong love affair with collecting. Among other highlights are a 14th-century carved ivory English hunting horn (Room 17); an ivory sceptre used by

Polish kings (Room 26); *Virgin with the Innocents* by Rubens and *Portrait of a Lady* by Rembrandt (Room 35); and a sensual portrait of *The Bather* by Renoir (Room 40). If you need a break to recharge your batteries, there is a café on the ground floor.

✚ 200 B2 ✉ Rooseveltov Trg 4
☎ 01 4828 100 ⏰ Tue–Wed, Fri–Sat 10–5, Thu 10–7, Sun 10–2 💰 Moderate

## ⑧ Etnografski Muzej

The last in the trio of museums on the western side of the "Green Horseshoe" (► panel below) is devoted to folk culture, both in Croatia and elsewhere. The ground-floor gallery of the Ethnographic Museum features objects brought back from abroad by Croatian explorers, notably the brothers **Mirko and Stjepan Seljan**. Of greater interest are the first-floor displays of folk costume and jewellery from the various regions of Croatia, along with a number of traditional musical instruments. The museum is housed in a magnificent congress hall, dating from 1904, with beautiful stained glass, sculptures on the facade and frescoes inside the central dome.

✚ 200 B2 ✉ Mažuranića trg 14
☎ 01 482 6220 ⏰ Tue–Thu 10–6, Fri–Sun 10–1 💰 Inexpensive (free on Thu)

**Ornate neo-Renaissance arcades of Groble Mirogoj**

### THE GREEN HORSESHOE
Glance at a map of *Donji Grad* (Lower Town) and you will easily make out the Green Horseshoe, a U-shaped promenade of interconnected parks and squares designed by Milan Lenuci (1849–1924). The aim was to provide a green lung for the expanding city, with parks for relaxation, along with handsome buildings housing the museums, art galleries and theatres where citizens could spend their leisure time. Although the horseshoe was never completed, two major sections are still in place today. The first begins on Trg Nikole Šubića Zrinskog and continues south to the equestrian statue of King Tomislav on Trg Kralja Tomislava, passing through Strossmayerova Trg, where you can find the Strossmayerova Galerija Starih Majstora (Strossmayer Gallery of Old Masters). A parallel section begins by the Hrvatsko Narodno Kazalište (Croatian National Theatre) on Trg Maršala Tita and leads south past the Ethnographic Museum towards the Botanički Vrt (Botanical Garden), an English-style landscape garden laid out in 1889.

### 9 Arheološki Muzej

Spread out over three floors of a 19th-century Habsburg palace, this archaeological museum has a comprehensive collection of finds from prehistoric to Roman times, but the biggest attraction is the Vučedol Dove, a three-legged pouring vessel in the shape of a bird dating from the third millennium BC. The vessel probably served some religious or ceremonial function, such as anointing with oil. It is the finest surviving example of the grooved pottery, decorated with geometric patterns, that was a hallmark of the

**Picturesque view of Medvednica (Bear Mountain) in midwinter**

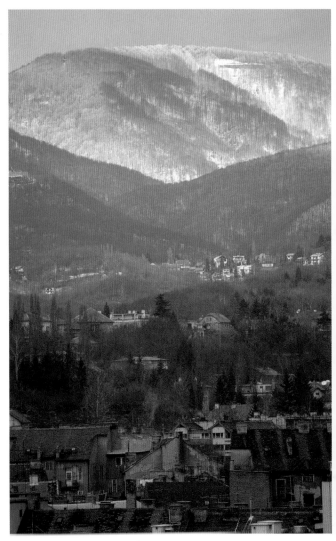

Vučedol culture around Vukovar in eastern Croatia more than 4,000 years ago. Since the siege of Vukovar in 1991, the Vučedol Dove has become a powerful symbol of peace, reproduced on the 20-kuna banknote. Also on display is the Zagreb Mummy, brought back from Egypt in 1848. It was wrapped in a 4th-century BC linen shroud containing the world's longest example of the Etruscan language – an ancient text still to be deciphered. Don't miss the Lapidarium in the museum courtyard, with Roman stone monuments and a café.

✚ 201 D3 ✉ Trg Nikole Šubića Zrinskog 19 ☎ 01 4873 101 ⏰ Tue, Wed, Fri 10–5, Thu 10–10, Sat–Sun 10–1 💵 Moderate

## 🔟 Maksimirski Perivoj

The residents of Zagreb flock to Maksimir Park, one of the oldest public parks in Europe, on weekend afternoons to stroll, ride bicycles, feed the swans, take the kids to play on the swings or relax on the grass. Footpaths, lakes, bridges, follies and a belvedere café all help to create an enjoyable retreat, a short tram ride from the city. A **zoo** houses native species such as brown bears and wolves, as well as elephants, lions, tigers, chimpanzees, crocodiles, an aquarium and a reptile house.

✚ 201 F3 🚋 Tram 4, 7, 11, 12

### Zoo

☎ 01 2302 199 ⏰ Daily 9–8, in summer; 9–5, in winter 💵 Moderate

## 1️⃣1️⃣ Medvednica

The wooded slopes of Medvednica (Bear Mountain) offer the nearest thing to a wilderness experience and make an excellent day-trip from Zagreb. Take tram 8 or 14 to the Mihaljevac terminus, from where you can take buses to the summit; the cable car has been suspended at the time of writing. Look for the entrance signs to the Medvednica nature park, walk through the tunnel and stay on a woodland path before climbing the steps to the *žičara* (cable-car) station.

From the summit of Sljeme at 1,035m (3,395feet), there are numerous walking trails in the beech woods, and you can even ski from the summit in winter. For an easy half-day excursion, turn right at the upper cable-car station and follow signs to Puntijarka to reach a large sloping meadow. Shortly afterwards you will come to the Church of Our Lady of Sljeme, built in 1932 at an altitude of 1,000m (3,280 feet) to celebrate 1,000 years of Christianity in Croatia. Stay on this path as far as the Puntijarka mountain refuge (➤ 62), then follow trail No 18 back down to Dolje through the woods.

✚ 201 D5 ⏰ Buses: daily every 1hr 30mins, 6:20am–9:50pm

## 1️⃣2️⃣ Groblje Mirogoj

Take the bus to Mirogoj from outside the cathedral and you will probably be joined by widows carrying flowers and candles to adorn their husbands' graves – a reminder that this is a real cemetery, not just a museum piece.

Designed by the ubiquitous Hermann Bollé in 1876, it lies behind a long ivy-covered wall topped with green domes. Most impressive are the neo-Renaissance arcades to either side of the main entrance, with mosaic-tiled floors and elaborate funereal monuments marking the tombs of Croatia's noble families.

Halfway along the arcade to the right, look out for the tomb of Stjepan Radić (1871–1928), the leader of the Croatian Peasants Party and advocate of independence who was shot dead in the Belgrade parliament in 1928. The first president of Croatia, Franjo Tuđman (1922–99), occupies a grandiose black granite tomb behind the main chapel. It's just as interesting to wander among the rows of ordinary graves, where Catholic, Orthodox, Jewish, Muslim and Communist citizens lie buried side by side, the symbols on their tombstones illustrating clearly that this is a cemetery for all the people of Zagreb.

✚ 201 D5 ⏰ Daily 8–6 🚌 106

# Where to... Stay

## Prices

Expect to pay per person per night for a double room in summer:

€ under 250kn   €€ 250kn–500kn   €€€ over 500kn

## Dubrovnik €€€

Built in 1929, the Dubrovnik is most notable for its rippling glass facade, which looks down over the pedestrianized shopping streets to the south of Trg Bana Jelačića. Some of the 260 rooms overlook the main square, all have air-conditioning and satellite TV. It's a good choice if you want to be at the heart of things, with the buzzing café life of Bogovićeva just a few steps away.

🕂 201 D3 ☒ Ulica Ljudevita Gaja 1
☎ 01 486 3555; www.hotel-dubrovnik.hr
🚃 Tram 1, 6, 11, 12, 13, 14, 17

## Ilica €€

This small, friendly hotel is set just back from a busy shopping street, a 15-minute walk from Trg Bana Jelačića. There are 20 cosy rooms with private bathrooms, and the corridors are decorated with impressions of Zagreb by local artists. Ilica is the best mid-range option in central Zagreb and it tends to get booked up, so reserve in advance. No credit cards; you can pay in euros or Croatian kuna.

🕂 200 A3 ☒ Ilica 102 ☎ 01 3777 522; www.hotel-ilica.hr 🚃 Tram 1, 6, 11

## Palace €€€

The grande dame of Zagreb hotels was built as the Schlessinger Palace in 1891 and converted to a hotel in 1907, the first hotel in the city. Despite renovation, it retains its old-world atmosphere and oozes art nouveau charm and antique style. Many of the rooms look over Strossmayerova Trg, a leafy square at the heart of the green corridor connecting the railway station with Trg Bana Jelačića.

🕂 201 D2 ☒ Strossmayerova Trg 10
☎ 01 4899 600; www.palace.hr
🚃 Tram 6, 13

## Regent Esplanade €€€

If you really want to do it in style, stay at the Esplanade, built in 1925 for passengers arriving on the Orient Express. Royalty, politicians and film stars have all slept here. Following renovation, the fountain in the gardens and the art deco lobby are still there, but modern business facilities and wireless internet access have been introduced, along with a health club and casino. Fresh flowers, marble bathrooms, walk-in showers, goose-down pillows and fluffy towels guarantee a stay here is the height of unashamed luxury. The botanical garden is a short stroll away.

🕂 201 D1 ☒ Ulica Mihanovićeva 1
☎ 01 4566 666; www.theregentzagreb.com
🚃 Tram 2, 4, 6, 9, 13

## Sliško €€

This small, modern, family-run hotel makes a convenient choice for anyone arriving by bus as it is just 200m (220 yards) from the bus station and the airport bus terminus. There are 18 simply furnished rooms, with private bathrooms and satellite TV. It stands in a quiet street, a 15-minute tram ride or 30-minute walk from Trg Bana Jelačića. Guests have free access to a computer in the lobby if they want to check their emails.

🕂 201 off F1 ☒ Ulica Supilova 13
☎ 01 6184 777; www.slisko.hr
🚃 Tram 2, 5, 6, 7, 8

# Where to...
## Eat and Drink

### Prices
Expect to pay for a starter, main course, salad and house wine or water for one:

€ under 100kn    €€ 100kn–200kn    €€€ over 200kn

### Baltazar €€
This long-established restaurant just north of the cathedral serves a classic menu of grilled meat dishes such as steaks, chops and burgers with a choice of chips, roasted peppers or potato balls with gorgonzola. It can get busy, so reserve ahead, especially if you want a table in the courtyard. If you have a Zagreb Card, remember to claim your 10 per cent discount. On the same site are Gašpar, a fish restaurant, and Melkior, a wine bar.

➕ 201 D4 ◻ Nova Ves 4 ☎ 01 4666 999
🕐 Mon–Sat noon–midnight 🚌 Bus 106

### Boban €€
The footballer Zvonimir Boban, captain of Croatia's 1998 World Cup squad, opened this Italian restaurant in a brick-vaulted cellar just off the main square. Fresh pasta is the house special here, with spaghetti, tortellini, ravioli and gnocchi prepared in a variety of ways, along with carpaccio of beef or tuna and Italian-inspired salads and risottos. The restaurant and the bar attract a young, trendy crowd.

➕ 201 D3 ◻ Ulica Ljudevita Gajeva 9
☎ 01 4811 549 🕐 Daily 11am–midnight
🚊 Tram 1, 6, 11, 12, 13, 14, 17

### Ivica i Marica €€
Ivica and Marica are Croatia's Hansel and Gretel, and this enjoyable restaurant on Zagreb's main bar-hopping strip combines a fairytale cottage atmosphere with light, healthy organic and vegetarian cuisine. There are a few meat and fish dishes, including trout from the Žumberak rivers, but most people stick to vegetarian choices such as goulash, wholemeal pasta and Štrukli (baked pastry parcels with cheese and spinach). However, if you just want a snack, choose from the delectable selection of home-made cakes at the pastry shop next door.

➕ 201 D4 ◻ Tkalčićeva 70
☎ 01 4817 321 🕐 Daily noon–11

### Korčula €€
Only one block south of the heart of Zagreb's café society, this is a well-regarded traditional restaurant that's smart enough to feel like dining out without any of the formalities. Foodwise, Korčula has a high-quality Dalmatian menu that is strong on seafood – fresh Adriatic fish served with blitva, octopus prepared in a peka – but also has room for rich beef stew pašticada.

➕ 200 D3 ◻ Nikole Tesle 17
☎ 01 4872 159 🕐 Mon–Sat 11am–11pm

### Kerempuh €€
This busy restaurant on the upper level of Dolac market attracts a mixed crowd of market workers, shoppers, business people and tourists, so try to arrive early for a lunchtime seat on the terrace. The menu changes daily according to what is available in the market, so the food is ultra-fresh and you have a prime view of the activity going on beneath you. The main emphasis is on meat dishes such as pašticada, a casserole of veal stewed in wine and served with mashed potatoes. Stuffed cabbage is another speciality at Kerempuh.

➕ 201 D3 ◻ Kaptol 3 ☎ 01 4819 000
🕐 Mon–Sat 9–3, 7–11, Sun 9–4
🚊 Tram 1, 6, 11, 12, 13, 14, 17

## Paviljon €€€

Paviljon occupies the ground floor of the Art Pavilion, an art nouveau building, originally designed for an international exhibition in Budapest in 1896, then reassembled two years later in Zagreb. With modern art on the walls and a pianist playing while you dine, this classy restaurant is definitely a place to dress up for that special occasion. The Paviljon's menu is a combination of Croatian, Italian and Central European influences, from the signature dish of crispy roast duck on a bed of red cabbage with figs to offerings such as tasty shrimps with chickpeas and rosemary or succulent chicken stuffed with truffles and Fontina cheese.

🚹 201 D2 ⊠ Trg Kralja Tomislava 22
☎ 01 4813 066 🕓 Mon–Sat noon–midnight
🚋 Tram 2, 4, 6, 9, 13

## Pod Gričkim Topom €€

Pod Gričkim Topom, whose name translates as 'under the Grič cannon', makes the perfect setting for a romantic meal. The attentive staff at this flower-decked terrace, overlooking Zagreb a few steps from the Lotrščak Tower, are fluent in several languages, and will bring you a small starter on the house. Afterwards, you could try the Zagorje soup, a hearty broth of ham, cheese, bacon, mushrooms and potatoes. The main menu is heavy on grilled fish and expertly cooked steaks, such as the *zagrebački odrezak*, a veal schnitzel stuffed with ham and cheese. If you need the toilet at Pod Gričkim Topom, remember that the key symbol is for men and the keyhole is for women.

🚹 200 C3 ⊠ Zakmardijeve Stube 5 (near upper funicular station) ☎ 01 4833 607
🕓 Mon–Sat 11am–midnight, Sun 11–5
🚋 Funicular to Gradec

## Puntijarka €

An easy 45-minute walk from the upper cable-car station leads to this mountain refuge on the slopes of Medvednica (Bear Mountain). There are no frills here, just good, hearty fare such as *grah* (bean stew), roast pork and *purica z mlincima* (turkey with pasta), served at outdoor tables in summer or in the smug alpine lodge in winter. A path beside the restaurant leads down towards the tram terminus at Dolje. This means you can easily come up to Puntijarka on the cable car for lunch and then walk back down in a couple of hours.

🚹 201 off D5 ⊠ Sljemenska Cesta 4
☎ 01 4580 384 🕓 Daily 9–9

## Rubelj €

Rubelj is the busiest of several cheap grill restaurants on a terrace beneath Dolac market, with enticing outdoor tables and giant parasols. The simple menu features *ćevapčići*, kebabs, hamburgers, sausages and mixed grills, served with a selection of crusty bread, raw onions and *djvar* (aubergine and pepper relish). Steaks, pizzas, grilled squid, salad and chips are all available, but most people go for the *ćevapčići*. This restaurant is a great place for a light, snack lunch, right in the heart of town.

🚹 201 D3 ⊠ Dolac 2 ☎ 01 4818 777
🕓 Daily 8am–11pm 🚋 Tram 1, 6, 11, 12, 13, 14, 17

## Vallis Aurea €

A little piece of Slavonia in the heart of Zagreb, Vallis Aurea lies at the foot of the funicular that leads to Gradec. The wooden tables and embroidered tablecloths give the restaurant a cosy, intimate atmosphere. The food is spicy, with starters such as ham and horse-radish, smoked ox tongue or *kulen* (Slavonian salami), and there are always three good-value daily specials ranging from boiled beef to fish stew. If you don't really fancy a full meal, why not enjoy a glass of chilled Slavonian wine outside on the summer terrace.

🚹 200 C3 ⊠ Ulica Tomića 4
☎ 01 4831 305 🕓 Mon–Sat 9am–11pm
🚋 Tram 1, 6, 11, 12, 13, 14, 17

# Where to... Shop

Shopping in Zagreb has come a long way since the days of Communist Yugoslavia, and the city now has a variety of department stores, fashion boutiques and shopping malls.

## SHOPPING CENTRES

Many of Zagreb's smarter shops are in shopping centres rather than on the main streets. Among the biggest are the historic department store **Nama** (Nova Ves 17), **Centar Kaptol** (Nova Ves 17), **Importanne** (Starčevićev Trg, outside the railway station) and **Importanne Galleria** (Iblerov Trg, near Vlaška).

The more modern centres, such as **Centar Kaptol** and **Importanne Galleria** (open Mon–Sat 9–9; some open Sunday), resemble American-style shopping malls, with eateries, multiplex cinemas, and shops.

## SHOPPING DISTRICTS

The main shopping areas are all close to Trg Bana Jelačića. **Ilica**, which runs 7km west of Trg Bana Jelačića for some 7km (4 miles), has been the city's main commercial street since the 19th century and now houses shops selling antiques, clothing and shoes. **Vlaška**, which begins near the cathedral and continues east, offers a similar mix.

For more alternative shopping, **Radićeva** and **Tkalčićeva**, running uphill from the northwest corner of Trg Bana Jelačića, have funky, offbeat designer boutiques and quirky art galleries and craft shops. **Arkadija** (Radićeva 35) specializes in carnival masks, while **Bil-Ani** (Radićeva 37) sells handmade miniatures of Croatian buildings.

## FOOD AND DRINK

For fresh produce, you can't beat the farmers' market which takes place every morning at Dolac, just off Trg Bana Jelačića. Fresh fruit and vegetables are displayed on outdoor stalls, while freshly baked bread, pasta, cheese, and fresh and cured meats are available inside the market hall.

A short walk east of the cathedral, **Franja** (Vlaška 62) sells fresh coffees and teas, plus a wide selection of wines and liqueurs. There is another branch of **Franja** on Ilica 24). **Vinoteka Bornstein** (Kaptol 19) is the place to go for Croatian wine, and it has a second outlet at Pantovčak 9. **Bakina Kuća** (Strossmayerova Trg 7) and **Natura Croatica** (Preradovićeva 8) sell tempting honeys, jams and liqueurs.

## FASHIONS

**Heruc Galerija** (Ilica 26) and **Image Haddad** (Ilica 6) are high-street chains offering affordable, stylish women's clothes. For something more glamorous, check out **Gharani Strok** (Dezmanova 5), owned by a London-based Croatian fashion designer.

**Croata** (Ilica 5 and Kaptol 13) is the place to pick up a Croatian silk tie for the man in your life.

## OTHER SHOPS

**Algoritam** (Ulica Ljudevita Gaja 1), beneath Hotel Dubrovnik, is the top bookshop in town, with foreign-language books and magazines, including Croatian literature translated into English.

**Aromatica** (Vlaška 7) is the place to go for cosmetics and soaps made naturally from Adriatic herbs.

# Where to...
# Be Entertained

**Zagreb has a thriving arts scene, and with numerous theatres, cinemas, concert halls and orchestras, there is something going on throughout the year.**

To find out what's on, pick up a copy of the monthly *Events and Performances* leaflet from the tourist office on Trg Bana Jelačića, or check the listings on their website (www. zagreb-touristinfo.hr). Another good source of information is the magazine *Zagreb in your Pocket*, available free from tourist offices, cafés and hotels (www. inyourpocket.com).

In summer look for outdoor events such as the **bandstand concerts** on Saturday mornings in Trg Nikole Šubića Zrinskog, south of Trg Bana Jelačića. During the **International Folklore Festival** in July, folk dancers perform in Trg Bana Jelačića, while the annual **Zagreb Summer Evenings** festival, also held in July, features chamber music concerts in the cathedral and the courtyards of Gornji Grad.

## THEATRE AND MUSIC

The prestige venue for drama, ballet and opera is the **Hrvatsko Narodno Kazalište** (Croatian National Theatre; tel: 01 4888 415; www. hnk.hr), an ostentatious, Habsburg-era opera house on Trg Maršala Tita opened by Emperor Franz Josef I in 1895. The theatre is home to the National Ballet and National Opera, but also plays host to visiting companies throughout the year. The box office is open Monday to Friday 10–7:30, Saturday 10–1, plus 90 minutes before all of the performances.

The other major venue is the **Vatroslav Lisinski concert hall** at Trg Stjepan Radića 4 (tel: 01 6121 166; www.lisinski.hr). Home to the Zagreb Philharmonic Orchestra, it also features jazz and other musical events.

Children might enjoy the shows performed at the **Zagrebačko Kazalište Lutaka** (Zagreb Puppet Theatre) on Trg Kralja Tomislava.

## CINEMA

Most major international films are shown shortly after their release, usually with subtitles. Two good central cinemas are **Broadway Tkalca** in the Centar Kaptol shopping centre, and the **Zagreb** on Trg Petra Preradovića. Listings of what is on can be found in the daily newspapers.

## NIGHTLIFE

For most locals, a night out, especially in summer, means finding a café and sitting out on the street. The most popular streets are Radićeva and Tkalčićeva north of Trg Bana Jelačića, and Gajeva and Bogovićeva to the south. The established place for serious clubbers is **Aquarius** (www. aquarius.hr), on the shores of Lake Jarun, 4km (2.5 miles) south of the city. For live music, check out **Sax** at Palmotićeva 22 (tel: 01 4872 836; www.sax-zg.hr).

## FOOTBALL

The city's top football team, Dinamo Zagreb (www.nk-dinamo.hr), plays at the **Maksimir Stadium** opposite Maksimir Park, which is also the venue for home games for the Croatian national team. Matches take place at weekends between August and May. Check for tickets in advance (tel: 01 2386 111).

# Inland Croatia

# Getting Your Bearings

Although most visitors to Croatia tend to stay in Zagreb and around the coast, to do so is to ignore about half of the country. The regions to the north, south and east of Zagreb offer a beguiling mix of scenery, historic towns and authentic rural life. Travel in inland Croatia is not always easy – the roads are slow, facilities are basic and the continuing effects of the war can be emotionally wearing – but it certainly has its rewards for the adventurous visitor who is prepared to step off the beaten track.

## ★ Don't Miss

## At Your Leisure

The rivers Sava, Drava and Danube form natural borders with Bosnia, Hungary and Serbia, separating Croatia from its neighbours. This entire region has long had the feel of a frontier land, ever since Pope Leo X declared Croatia to be "the ramparts of Christendom" in 1519. During the 16th century, the Habsburg emperors established a military frontier along the Bosnian border in order to defend Croatia from the Turks. Four centuries later, the same border became a battleground and the scars of the recent war are still evident in towns such as Osijek, Slavonski Brod and especially Vukovar.

The eastern province of Slavonia, virtually untouched by tourism, is a region of vineyards, wheat fields and villages, where people sell sacks of red peppers from outside their houses, which end up in the famously spicy salami, goulash and fish stew. The chic resorts of Istria and Dalmatia seem a very long way away.

**Page 65:**
**Flower cart rests against a typical baroque building in Varazdin**

**Below: Visitors to Plitvice National Park enjoying a boat tour on one of the lakes**

# In Four Days

If you're not quite sure where to begin your travels, this itinerary recommends an enjoyable four-day tour of inland Croatia, taking in some of the best places to see using the Getting Your Bearings map on the previous page. The attractions are spread across a wide area and this tour involves many hours of driving on country roads, so you need to be prepared for long days.

## Day 1

### Morning
Make an early start to explore ❶ **Plitvička Jezera** (left, ➤ 70). You could easily spend all day here, but in a few hours you should be able to walk to the Veliki Slap waterfall and take a boat trip across Lake Kozjak.

### Afternoon and Evening
Head north along the old main road from Split to Zagreb, where several rustic roadside restaurants offer spit-roast lamb and pork. Arriving at Karlovac, take the minor road to Jastrebarsko and drive over the hills to spend the night in ❻ **Samobor** (➤ 82). If you still have some room, the cafés around the main square serve custard tarts.

## Day 2

### Morning
Take the motorway towards Zagreb, then north to Zabok to begin a circuit of the Zagorje with the small museum village of ❼ **Kumrovec** (➤ 82).

### Afternoon and Evening
After lunch at Grešna Gorica (➤ 87), you should just have time to visit the ❷ **Zagorje Castles** of Veliki Tabor and Trakošćan (right, ➤ 73–75) before continuing to the baroque town of ❸ **Varaždin** (➤ 76–77). Take an evening walk around the old town and have a drink in the main square before a slap-up dinner at Zlatna Guška (➤ 87).

# Day 3

## Morning

It takes about three hours to drive across the Pannonian plain from Varaždin to Osijek, though you could break the journey with a visit to the naïve art galleries of **8 Hlebine** (➤ 83).

## Afternoon and Evening

Arriving in Osijek (➤ 83), head straight for the **4 Kopački Rit** Nature Park (➤ 78–79) and book a boat trip on the *Orao I* to see herons and cormorants on the Danube flood plain. Spend the night in the nearby village of Bilje (Mala Kuća ➤ 85) and treat yourself to some spicy Slavonian stew at Kod Varge (➤ 87).

# Day 4

## Morning

Spend an hour wandering around the Tvrđa, the 18th-century fortress on the outskirts of Osijek, then head south to **11 Đakovo** (➤ 84) to see the magnificent cathedral.

## Afternoon and Evening

Join the main Zagreb-Belgrade motorway for the fast journey to Novska, drive south to Jasenovac, the entry point for the **5 Lonjsko Polje** Nature Park (above, ➤ 80–81). Spend the the day exploring the villages inside the park, then stay the night in a wooden cottage at Mužilovčica (➤ 85).

# Plitvička Jezera

The Plitvice Lakes are undoubtedly inland Croatia's top tourist attraction, seen by more than 600,000 visitors a year. In 1949, the entire area was declared Croatia's first national park, and in 1979 it was given UNESCO World Heritage status. In summer, it is crowded with coach parties from the coastal resorts, but come out of season, or early in the morning and you can still have the place to yourself.

There can be no more dramatic sight in Croatia than the rushing waters of **Veliki Slap**, cascading 70m (230 feet) over a limestone cliff and into the **River Korana**. This is merely the culmination of a series of 16 emerald-green lakes, linked by waterfalls, which drop more than 150m (490 feet) over a distance of 8km (5 miles). Marked paths and wooden bridges take you through the park.

The lakes were formed from travertine, a muddy, calcareous deposit left behind by the mixture of moss and eroded limestone, with the result that they are gradually rising. This is a rare, lush landscape in a region where rugged limestone karst is the dominant feature. Brown bears and wolves inhabit the beech, fir and spruce forests, and lynx have returned.

Numerous species of butterflies, birds and wild flowers thrive here. The peaceful scenes of nature are tragically at odds with the recent history of the park – it was occupied by Serb forces from 1991 to 1995 and the first deaths in the war occurred here.

## Seeing the Lakes

It is possible to spend several days exploring the national park, staying at one of the **three on-site hotels**, but most people come just for a day trip. Even if you only have a few hours, the park is so well geared up for visitors that you can easily make the most of your time. The lakes are connected by a network of **wooden footpaths** and **bridges**, some of which pass right under and across the waterfalls, close enough to feel the spray.

With constantly changing colours and light, the Plitvice Lakes take on a different character in each season of the year. In summer, when most visitors come, they are refreshingly cool but crowded. The best times to visit are spring, when melting snows increase the flow of water, and autumn, when the forests take on a gorgeous hue. In winter, when the park is almost deserted, the lakes have a special atmosphere, but they are often covered in snow and ice.

## Getting Around

The entrance ticket (valid for one day, but can be extended) also includes access to **boat trips** and **shuttle bus services**. The maps sold at the entry points and hotels suggest a variety

**The lakes at Plitvička Jezera are connected by winding wooden footpaths and bridges**

of itineraries from two to six hours, using a combination of walking and free transport. In four hours, starting from Entrance 1, you could follow the blue trail to **Veliki Slap** and take a boat across the largest lake, **Jezero Kozjak**, before returning on the bus. If you have a full day, start at Entrance 2 and take a bus to the **Labudovac Falls** at the head of the highest lake, Prošćansko. From here you can follow the red trail along the shores to **Jezero Kozjak** and take the boat trip downstream, saving Veliki Slap till last. With the map and the well-signed paths, it is easy to work out your own route and itinerary.

## TAKING A BREAK

There are cafés by the park entrances and also at the major boat and bus stops in the summer.

For a full meal, the rustic **Lička Kuća restaurant** at Entrance 1 (tel: 053 751 024, open Apr–Oct times are the same as the park) serves traditional local dishes. In winter, the only options for a place to eat are the hotels (➤ 86).

**Above:** Marked paths in Plitvička Jezera lead right up to the stunning waterfalls

**Right:** View of the Gothic castle at Veliki Tabor

+ 193 F3
✉ 75km (47 miles) south of Karlovac
☎ 053 751 015; www.np-plitvicka-jezera.hr
🕐 Summer daily 8–8 (or dusk); winter 8–3
💲 Expensive (varies from 110kn in summer to 70kn in winter)

---

## PLITVIČKA JEZERA: INSIDE INFO

**Top tips** If you only have a few hours to explore, **it is worth spending the previous night in one of the on-site hotels** and making an early start before the coach parties arrive.

■ The **entry fee is lower in winter**, but the boats and shuttle buses stop operating in November and the paths may be closed due to snow. However, you might catch a glimpse of Veliki Slap from the observation point near Ulaz 1.

**In more depth** There are **two main entrances**, Ulaz 1 and Ulaz 2, both with parking areas and information offices. Ulaz 1 is the nearest to Veliki Slap, just 50m (55 yards) from an observation terrace overlooking the falls. Ulaz 2 is closer to the three hotels and makes a good starting point if you want to explore the upper lakes and waterfalls.

# ② Zagorje Castles

Vineyards, meadows and rolling green hills topped by picture-book castles and churches – the Zagorje region north of Zagreb is one of the most attractive in Croatia.

## Veliki Tabor

This 16th-century Gothic castle, built on a hill 333m (1,092 feet) high, completely dominates its surroundings, though it is more impressive from a distance than close-up, as it is undergoing long-term renovation. The basic structure is pentagonal, with four semicircular towers set around an arcaded courtyard, where occasional displays of swordmanship and falconry are held. The **museum** contains a fairly dull collection of archaeological finds, but it is worth the entrance fee for the views over the Zagorje in all directions.

## Trakošćan

The most visited sight in the Zagorje is the site of the original **13th-century castle**, built to defend the Bednja valley at the border with Slovenia. Trakošćan comes straight out of a fairytale, with gleaming white walls and crenellated

---

**THE STORY OF VERONIKA**
The first castle at Veliki Tabor was built in the 12th century for the counts of Celje. A local tale recounts the legend of Veronika of Desinić, who fell in love with the count's son and secretly eloped with him to Slovenia, where they married. When she was captured, the count had her imprisoned and later ordered her to be drowned and her body walled into the castle. A female skull was found here in 1982 — before renovation of the galleried courtyard, it was on display in the chapel — though nobody knows whether it is Veronika's.

towers looking down over an artificial lake. The castle you see today is the result of a 19th-century restoration by the **Draškovič family**, descendants of a 16th-century noble who was granted the estate by the Habsburg emperor as a reward for fighting against the Turks. Cross the drawbridge and climb the path up the wooded hillside to enter the castle, a fine example of an aristocratic stately home with tapestries, paintings, armour, hunting trophies, a music salon, smoking and gaming rooms and some splendid 18th-century braziers.

Also, here is the study of **Julijana Erdödy-Drašković** (1847–1901), the first recognized female painter in Croatia, who lived here in the 19th century; her original piano and easel are preserved, and the room is decorated with her

Religious artefacts on sale at the pilgrimage town of Marija Bistrica

### MARIJA BISTRICA

While you are in the Zagorje, visit Marija Bistrica, the **most important pilgrimage site in Croatia**. The object of veneration here is a 15th-century dark wooden statue of the Virgin, said to have been hidden by the priest in the walls of the parish church to protect it from Turkish invaders, and rediscovered in 1684 when a shining light directed the bishop to its hiding place. The current church dates from 1883 and was the work of Hermann Bollé (1845–1916), the architect of Zagreb cathedral, who incorporated an earlier stone gateway and facade into its design. You enter through Trg Pape Ivana Pavla II, named in honour of Pope John Paul II's visit in 1998, with a half-cloister featuring a pair of domed pavilions and numerous marble *ex votos* or prayers of thanks left by previous pilgrims. Climb the **Via Crucis** (Way of the Cross) behind the church for the best views. On **religious feast days,** particularly 15 August (Assumption) and 8 September (Birth of the Virgin), Marija Bistrica has a **fairground atmosphere,** with stalls selling popcorn, balloons and gingerbread hearts, and thousands of pilgrims attending open-air Mass in the auditorium behind the church.

paintings of rural life. After exploring the castle, you can walk around the lake. In summer there is a **lakeside café** where you can rent a pedal-boat for a trip on the water.

**TAKING A BREAK**

Have lunch or a drink on the terrace of **Grešna Gorica** (➤ 87), looking out over the castle at Veliki Tabor.

Sheaves of wheat in the rural landscape of Zagorje

**Veliki Tabor**
➕ 194 B4 ☎ 049 343 963 🕐 Summer daily 9–5; winter 9–3 ✋ Inexpensive

**Trakošćan**
➕ 194 B4 ☎ 042 796 422 🕐 Summer daily 9–6; winter 9–4
💳 Moderate

## ZAGORJE CASTLES: INSIDE INFO

**In more depth** Midway between Veliki Tabor and Trakošćan is the town of **Krapina**, best known for the discovery of *Homo Krapinensis*, a Neanderthal person who lived here some 30,000 years ago. Around 900 human bones were discovered on the Hušnjakovo hill, representing more than 10 men, women and children, the richest collection of prehistoric human remains found anywhere. The **Museum of Evolution** (summer daily 9–5, winter 9–3) features reproductions of Neanderthal skulls and the full skeleton of a cave bear. You can also walk up the hill behind the museum to see where the remains were discovered. A new, interactive museum is planned for this site, opening in autumn 2009.

# ③ Varaždin

The town of Varaždin is all pretty pastel shades and heavily restored facades in apricot, strawberry and vanilla, adorned with baroque angels and garlands of flowers. It's a gem of a place, supremely self confident and beautifully well kept, full of students on bicycles, artists, musicians, outdoor cafés and cobbled streets.

Founded in the 12th century, Varaždin briefly became the capital of Croatia from 1756 to 1776, until much of the town was destroyed by a fire. The result of rebuilding is a harmonious ensemble of baroque palaces and churches, whose onion-shaped domes and towers dominate the skyline.

This is a town for gentle strolling, especially among the traffic-free streets of the centre, looking out for hidden details, from secret courtyards to coats of arms above the doors. Sooner or later you will come to the main square, **Trg Kralja Tomislava**, with its 16th-century town hall topped by an 18th-century clock tower.

**Be sure to visit Stari Grad in the relaxed town of Varaždin**

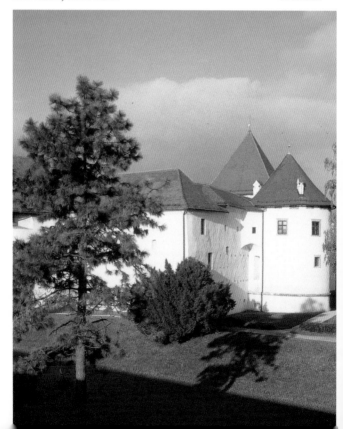

## Stari Grad

The one must-see sight is Stari Grad, part castle, part manor house, reached across a drawbridge and set in its own small park, surrounded by grassy ramparts and a dried-up moat. This whitewashed, red-roofed fortress, with a beautiful three-tiered courtyard in the middle, is home to the **city museum**.

The first-floor galleries feature the town magistrate's mace and seal from 1464, as well as the original Gothic gateway to the castle. The second-floor rooms are arranged thematically to give an idea of changing aristocratic tastes in furniture, from 16th-century Renaissance to early 20th-century art nouveau. Don't miss the **Kapelica Svetog Lovre** (Chapel of St Lawrence), reached along a first-floor balcony, and the adjoining sacristy, set inside a round defensive tower.

A room off the courtyard features stone sculpture from Varaždin, including a 17th-century figure of the Virgin and an 18th-century pillar with carved reliefs of saints, which once stood on the pilgrim route to Marija Bistrica.

## Groblje

When arriving by car, look for signs to the **Groblje** (cemetery), 500m (550 yards) west of the castle, where there is a large, free, parking area. Take a stroll around the cemetery, one of the most attractive in Croatia, laid out by Herman Haller in 1905.

### TAKING A BREAK

**Ritz** (tel: 042 312 830, open Sun–Thu 9am–11pm, Fri– Sat 9am–1am, inexpensive), on the corner of the main square is a popular coffee house with a rear courtyard and a cellar lounge bar. The outdoor terrace makes a great place for people-watching during the evening *korzo*.

---

➕ 194 C5
**Tourist Information Office**
✉ Ulica Ivana Padovca 3 ☎ 042 210 987

**Stari Grad**
☎ 042 212 918 🕐 May–Sep Tue–Sun 10–6; Oct–Apr Tue–Fri 10–5, Sat–Sun 10–1 💵 Moderate

### VARAŽDIN: INSIDE INFO

**Top tip** Look out for the **Changing of the Guard**, which takes place on Saturday mornings at 11am in summer. The ceremony dates back to the 18th century and features the Purgari (Civil Guard), in their distinctive blue uniforms and bearskin hats.

**Ones to miss** The **Galerija Starih i Novih Majstora** (Gallery of Old and New Masters), in the 17th-century Sermage Palace outside the castle gates, can be omitted if you are short of time. The **Entomološki Muzej** (Entomological Museum), a collection of insects housed in the Herzer Palace, will also be of limited interest to most people. Opening times are the same as the castle.

# ④ Kopački Rit

This vast, beautiful wetland reserve at the confluence of the rivers Danube and Drava is an important refuge for large numbers of nesting and migrant birds.

The Danube flood plain is one of the most significant wetland habitats in Europe, but more than 80 per cent was lost during the 20th century as a result of building and overdevelopment.

The remaining area is spread over three different countries (Croatia, Hungary and Serbia), with varying degrees of protection. Around 180sq km (70sq miles) of the Kopački Rit wetlands were declared a nature park in 1967, but from 1991 to 1995 they were occupied by Serbian forces who laid landmines in the park. Fortunately, most of the wildlife has survived, the mines have been cleared and the area is once again safe for visitors.

Even on a short visit to Kopački Rit, you will see a wide variety of fauna and flora. Much of the park is made up of willow, poplar and oak forests, home to large populations of deer, pine marten and wild boar. The rivers teem with carp, pike and catfish, and the ponds of reed, sedge and waterlilies become great marshy swamps when the Danube floods in the summer months.

The best introduction to the park is to take a **boat trip** on the *Orao I*, which leaves three or four times daily between March and November from a jetty close to the visitor office. The staff issue you with binoculars, and you may see herons, cormorants and geese, or if you are lucky, even catch a glimpse of a kingfisher, white-tailed eagle or black stork.

Another option is to go walking in the oak forests around **Tikveš**, deep inside the park. The hunting lodge here was used by Prince Eugene of Savoy during the 18th century, and later by President Tito.

## TAKING A BREAK

There are two restaurants in Kopački Rit, both of which serve the local delicacy of carp roasted on a stick. The first restaurant is **Kormoran** (tel: 031 753 099) and is located 4km (2.5 miles) from the Podunavlje park entrance, while the second, **Tikveš** (tel: 031 752 901) can be found by the Tikveš castle.

Picturesque sunset over the wetlands of Kopački Rit

🞣 197 E4
☎ 031 752 320; www.kopacki-rit.com  🕐 Daily 8–4
🎫 Park entrance: inexpensive. Boat trip: expensive

---

## KOPAČKI RIT: INSIDE INFO

**Top tip** The **main entrance** to the park is near the village of **Kopačevo**. Head north from Osijek on the main road towards Hungary and turn right at the crossroads in Bilje, then follow signs to the park. There is a large parking area and a visitor office at the entrance.

■ Take binoculars, good walking shoes and insect repellent as **mosquitoes can be a problem**, especially in summer.

**In more depth** The nearby village of Kopačevo contains some good examples of **vernacular architecture**, with Hungarian-style houses built end-on to the road, their long galleries facing towards inner courtyards. This is part of the **Baranja**, a fertile region with close links to Hungary; to explore it in more detail, take the **Vinska Cesta (Wine Route)** north from Bilje through the villages of Kneževi Vinogradi, Suza and Zmajevac.

# ⑤ Lonjsko Polje

The villages of the Lonjsko Polje Nature Park, less than
100km (62 miles) from Zagreb, provide a peaceful escape
from the capital, with their picturesque wooden cottages,
forest walks and nesting storks in spring and summer.

The Lonjsko Polje occupies an area of around 500sq km
(193sq miles) on the flood plains of the River Sava and its
tributaries. Much of this area is made up of lowland oak
forest, while the remainder is pasture meadows, which turn
into marshy swamps whenever the rivers rise. The flood
waters attract numerous frogs and fish, which in turn provide
food for visiting waterfowl and white storks. Sturdy Posavina
horses graze on the pasturelands, and local farmers keep
spotted Turopolje pigs, a rare breed which feeds off acorns
and lives in the oak forests throughout the year.

Horses graze
in the
meadows of
Lonjsko Polje
Nature Park

The main route through the Lonjsko Polje follows the old
road from Sisak to Jasenovac, on the east bank of the Sava.
The road passes through many pretty villages, but if you only
have time for two, they should be **Čigoć** and **Krapje**.

## Čigoć

Čigoć has been designated the first **European Stork Village**
because of its large numbers of white storks, which nest here

in spring and can usually be seen between April and August. Virtually every house in the village has a stork's nest on the roof. The information office issues maps of waymarked walks, including a short stroll through the forest and a two-hour walk from Čigoć across the flood dike. The Sučić ethnographic museum, included in the park entry ticket, has a collection of domestic and farming artefacts from the late 19th and early 20th centuries.

Jasenovac concentration camp memorial, Lonjsko Polje

## Krapje

Krapje, 30km (18 miles) from Čigoć, is an "architectural heritage" village with a fine collection of traditional wooden houses, and farm buildings. Several are being restored to create the new headquarters of the nature park.

The typical Posavina oak cottages are built end-on to the road, with external wooden staircases up to the living quarters on the first floor. They do not have chimneys; instead, the smoke is allowed to escape through the roof timbers and the attic is used for curing meat.

Just outside Krapje is **Krapje Đol**, Croatia's first ornithological reserve when it opened in 1963 and a haven for waterfowl, including herons, egrets and spoonbill. If you are interested in guided walks ask at the information office for further details.

### TAKING A BREAK

There are no restaurants in the Lonjsko Polje Nature park, but tasty farmhouse cooking is available at **Rastovac** (Čigoć 44; tel: 044 715 321) and **Ravlić**, the family owned cottage in Mužilovčica (➤ 85).

✚ 195 D3
**Information Office**
✉ Čigoć 26 ☎ 044 715 115; www.pp-lonjsko-polje.hr
🕐 Daily 8–4 💶 Park: moderate

# At Your Leisure

## 6 Samobor

When the people of Zagreb want a weekend in the country, they go to Samobor. Just 20km (12.5 miles) west of the capital, this is the perfect provincial town, with handsome 19th-century town houses around an elongated main square, overlooked by an onion-domed church. The pretty **Gradna** brook runs beneath the church, criss-crossed by wooden bridges in an area known as **Mala Venecija** (Little Venice).

An easy climb from the middle of town leads to a ruined 13th-century castle from the days of Samobor's establishment as a "royal free market town" with a charter from King Bela IV in 1242. More serious hikers can head for the **Žumberak-Samoborsko Gorje** Nature Park, a lovely region of forested hills and alpine meadows between Samobor and the Slovenian border.

If all that walking gives you an appetite, the cafés around the main square specialize in *samoborska kremšnita*, a flaky custard tart.

➕ 194 B3

**Tourist Information Office**

✉ Trg Kralja Tomislava 5 ☎ 01 3360 044

## 7 Kumrovec

This small village on the Slovenian border is best known as the birthplace of the Yugoslav leader Josip Broz Tito, born in 1892.

The house in which he was born was turned into a museum during his lifetime, but since his death more than 40 old buildings in the village have been reconstructed to give an idea of rural life in the Zagorje at the end of the 19th century and the conditions in which Tito grew up. The **Staro Selo** ethnographic museum is part of the modern village, with farmers on tractors, children on bicycles and families living in village houses alongside the exhibits. There are old farmsteads, granaries and stables, restored potters' and toymakers' studios and a reconstruction of the blacksmith's workshop once owned by Tito's parents. A statue of Tito marks the entrance to his birthplace, which now houses a display of old photos and uniforms.

A short walk down the main street leads to the school he attended from 1900 to 1905. In summer, there are exhibitions of rural crafts inside the various buildings and tastings of

**Birthplace of Josip Broz Tito, born in 1892, in the small village of Kumrovec**

Zagorje food in the old wine cellar
Zagorska Klet.
🚩 194 B4

**Staro Selo**
☎ 049 225 830 🕐 Apr–Sep daily 9–7;
Oct–Mar 9–4 💶 Moderate

## 8 Hlebine

Set in the fertile Podravina region,
close to the Hungarian border, the
village of Hlebine is considered
the birthplace of Croatian naïve art
(➤ 54) and has been home to more
than 200 painters and sculptors since
the 1930s. The **Galerija Hlebine**,
established in 1968, features
changing displays by contemporary
village artists, but also has a
permanent room devoted to Ivan
Generalić (1914–92), showing his
development from early portraits
and depictions of rural life to
fantastic visions of the Eiffel Tower
and Christ crucified among the
winter snows of Hlebine.
🚩 195 D4

**Galerija Hlebine**
✉ Trg Ivana Generalića 15 ☎ 048 836 075
🕐 Mon–Fri 10–4, Sat 10–2 💶 Inexpensive

## 9 Osijek

The capital of Slavonia lies on the
south bank of the River Drava,
roughly 30km (18 miles) from both
Hungary and Serbia. The heart of
the city is in Gornji Grad (Upper
Town), dominated by its 19th-
century red-brick cathedral, but
almost everything else of interest is
in the 18th-century Austrian fortress
of Tvrđa, 2km (1.2 miles) to the east.
You can get there by walking along
the riverbank promenade or taking
tram No 1 along Europska Avenija, a
grand park-lined boulevard linking
Tvrđa with Gornji Grad. Osijek
suffered heavy bombardment in
1991 and the damage is still visible,
but Tvrđa has recovered its easygoing
atmosphere, with students spilling
out of university faculties into the
cafés on the main square. The
square is lined with baroque palaces
and military buildings, with a

Plague monument in the centre of the
Tvrda area, Osijek

plague column dating from 1729 in
the middle.
   For the best views of Tvrđa, follow
the riverside path and cross the
elegant suspension bridge to the
town beach of Copacabana, then
return along the north bank and over
the road bridge, from where the full
extent of the fortress town is clear.
🚩 197 D3

**Tourist Information Office**
✉ Županijska 2 ☎ 031 203 755

## 10 Vukovar

Nowhere else in Croatia symbolizes
the horror of war as starkly as
Vukovar. During the 1990s, the town
became a byword for suffering, and
its name still strikes an emotional
chord with every Croat. Once a
prosperous market town on the west
bank of the Danube, with a mixed
Serbian and Croatian population and
some delightful baroque architecture,
Vukovar became a battleground
when it came under siege from
Serbian forces for three months in
1991. At least 2,000 people died
during the siege and many more
were killed afterwards and buried in
mass graves by the victorious Serbian
paramilitaries. An eerie silence hangs

**Buildings in town of Vukovar, ravaged by war**

over the town today, and few of the surviving Croats have returned.

The baroque Eltz Palace, with shell marks on its facade, is home to the town museum, but has been stripped of most of its treasures. A monument by the river, at the confluence of the Vuka and Danube and within sight of Serbia on the far bank, remembers the victims of war.

Just outside town on the road to Ilok, beyond the ruined shell of the old water tower, a cemetery contains row upon row of unmarked white crosses in memory of the bodies that were never found. Some of the atrocities committed in Vukovar are only just coming to light. This is not a place to linger, but a visit here can prompt sober reflections on the tragedy of war. The town of Ilok was also occupied during the war, but has returned to producing some of Croatia's best white wines, such as Graševina and Traminac.

➕ 197 E3

**Tourist Information Office**
✉ Strossmayerova 15  ☎ 032 442 889

## ⬛ Đakovo

This central Slavonian city is notable chiefly for its imposing red-brick cathedral, built by Bishop Josip Strossmayer between 1866 and 1882.

The bishop of Đakovo was a leading figure in 19th-century Croatian history and an early advocate of the concept of Yugoslavia. With twin spires rising to 84m (275 feet), the magnificent cathedral dominates the city completely. The interior is equally impressive, with frescoes, painted ceilings and a central cupola. The tomb of Bishop Strossmayer lies in the cathedral crypt.

A short walk from Đakovo's impressive cathedral leads to Ulica Hrvatskih Velikana, which is a pleasant café-lined promenade. Another attraction in Đakovo is the Lipizzaner stud farm and this is where the famous pure-white horses are bred.

➕ 197 D3

**Tourist Information Office**
✉ Ulica Kralja Tomislava 3  ☎ 031 812 319

---

**FOR KIDS**
- The **waterfalls** at the Plitvice Lakes (➤ 70–72).
- The **castle** at Trakošćan (➤ 73–74) – especially taking a pedal-boat onto the lake.
- The **boat trip** at Kopački Rit (➤ 78–79).
- **Storks** at Lonjsko Polje in summer (➤ 80–81).
- The **ethno-village** at Kumrovec (➤ 82–83).

# Where to... Stay

**Prices**

Expect to pay per person per night for a double room in summer:

€ under 250kn    €€ 250kn–500kn    €€€ over 500kn

## KOPAČKI RIT

### Mala Kuća €

An alternative to staying in one of the big hotels in Osijek when visiting Kopački Rit is to try private accommodation offered by several families in the nearby village of Bilje. Set just back from the main road in a quiet residential street, Mala Kuća has two rooms in the family home and four in a garden annexe, all with TV and shower. The friendly landlady will cook you dinner for a modest extra charge and also serves up huge breakfasts of home-made bread, eggs, bacon and potato cakes, all included in the price.

🕂 197 D4 ⊠ Ritska 1, Bilje
🕾 031 750 393; www.malakuca.com

### Sklepić €

Farmer Denis Sklepić has converted some of his farm buildings into comfortable bed-and-breakfast accommodation in the village of Karanac, 20km (12.5 miles) north of Bilje. With log fires, antique wooden beds, traditional cooking and horse and carriage rides, a stay here gives a real taste of rural Croatia. The village lies on a wine route in the region of Baranja, close to the Hungarian border.

🕂 197 D4 ⊠ Kolodvorska 58, Karanac
🕾 031 720 271; www.sklepic.hr

## LONJSKO POLJE

### Ravlić €

The Ravlić family welcomes visitors to their 200-year-old oak cottage, overlooking a lake on the old course of the River Sava in the village of Mužilovčica. Wooden steps lead up to a balcony and the guest room on the first floor, with its wooden beds, antique furniture and fading black-and-white photos. Geese, ducks and chickens run around the yard and the family also keep Turopolje pigs. Busy professionals from Zagreb drive out here at weekends for a back-to-nature experience, enjoying long farmhouse lunches in the garden. The Ravlić family have won awards for their pioneering approach to rural tourism. Horseback riding, fishing and boating on the lake can all be arranged, and dormitory beds are available in the old stables.

🕂 195 D3 ⊠ Mužilovčica 72
🕾 044 710 151

## OSIJEK

### Waldinger €€

This charming hotel, named after the 19th-century painter Adolf Waldinger, occupies an art nouveau building facing the Croatian National Theatre. With just 16 rooms and tasteful public areas, it is both intimate and stylish. Most of the rooms have Jacuzzis, and there is also a sauna and gym. The Viennese-style café on the ground floor hosts regular art exhibitions and has the feel of a literary salon from Austro-Hungarian Osijek. If you want something less expensive, there is a small pension (€) in the garden, with six simply furnished, comfortable, good-value rooms.

🕂 197 D3 ⊠ Županijska 8
🕾 031 250 450; www.waldinger.hr

## PLITVIČKA JEZERA

### Jezero €€€

The mountain lodge of Jezero overlooks Lake Kozjak and is the largest and most comfortable of the three national park hotels. There are 229 rooms, including 15 specially adapted for visitors with disabilities. Despite its get-away-from-it-all setting, there are tennis courts, a health centre, sauna, nightclub, children's playroom and business facilities. Also, all of the rooms have internet connections and satellite TV.

✚ **194 B1** ⊠ **Near Entrance 2**
☎ **053 751 400; www.np-plitvicka-jezera.hr**

## SAMOBOR

### Livadić €

This 19th-century town house on the main square is now a delightful family-run hotel, whose spacious, comfortable rooms are filled with antique furniture, rugs and parquet floors. The breakfast room, with its luxurious drapes and high-backed chairs, offers a daily feast of scrambled eggs, cold meats, yogurt, fresh fruit and delectable pastries, while the attached café (▶ 87) is the best place to try the local custard tarts. The whole place oozes taste and character, transporting you back to the last days of the Austro-Hungarian empire.

✚ **194 B3** ⊠ **Trg Kralja Tomislava 1**
☎ **01 3365 850; www.hotel-livadic.hr**

## VARAŽDIN

### Maltar €

There are only five places to stay in central Varaždin, and this small, friendly pension above a café offers perhaps the best value, with 15 functional, but comfortable rooms. There is a large parking area at the back of the café, and the centre of town is just a short walk away. Breakfast is served daily from 6am to noon.

✚ **194 C5** ⊠ **Ulica Prešernova 1**
☎ **042 311 100; www.maltar.hr**

## VUKOVAR

### Lav €€

It is unlikely that you will want to stay long in Vukovar, but at least there is now a comfortable hotel if you should find yourself here late in the day and need to spend the night. The Hotel Lav was originally built in 1840 and has been destroyed by war three times, most recently during the siege of 1991. In February 2005, a new privately owned hotel opened on the ruins of the old building, with 42 rooms and four luxury apartments overlooking the River Danube.

✚ **197 E3** ⊠ **Strossmayerova 18**
☎ **032 445 100; www.hotel-lav.hr**

## ZAGORJE

### Lojzekova Hiža €

This traditional farmhouse near Marija Bistrica is a good example of the growing trend towards rural tourism in the Zagorje. It has nine cosy rooms in the attic, with sloping roofs and creaking wooden floors. Ducks and turkeys scrabble around in the yard and a stream runs through the garden. The owners make their own wine, spirits and jams. Horseback riding and bicycle rental are available.

✚ **194 C4** ⊠ **Gusakovec 116, 6km (4 miles) west of Marija Bistrica** ☎ **049 469 325; www.lojzekovahiza.com**

### Vuglec Breg €€€

A sophisticated agrotourism retreat among the Zagorje wine hills. The four cottages of this former hilltop hamlet 4km (2.5 miles) north of Krapinske Toplice were modernized in 2006 to create charming apartments with mod cons. The classy restaurant, Pri Kleti, prepares top-notch regional dishes and is frequently besieged on summer weekends by Zagreb's movers and shakers. A wine cellar offers tastings of the estate wines and there's tennis and riding facilities for guests.

✚ **194 B4** ⊠ **Škarićevo 151, Lepajci** ☎ **049 345 015; www.vuglec-breg.hr**

# Where to...
# Eat and Drink

## Prices

Expect to pay for a starter, main course, salad and house wine or water, for one:
€ under 100kn  €€ 100kn–200kn  €€€ over 200kn

## KOPAČKI RIT

### Kod Varge €

At the rustic Kod Varge, traditional Slavonian dishes focus on carp, catfish and perch from local rivers. There is also an excellent *kulen* (salami) and spicy *fiš paprikaš* (fish stew).

+ 197 D4 ⊠ Ulica Kralja Zvonimira 37A, Bilje ☎ 031 750 120 ❷ Daily 9am–11pm

## OSIJEK

### Slavonska Kuća €€

On the edge of the fortified Tvrda district, this folksy tavern has wooden benches and hunting and fishing trophies on the walls. The food is typically Slavonian, though one unusual offering is a starter of *riblja kobasica* (smoked fish sausage). Otherwise, it is best to stick to the classics dishes on the menu, such as *čobanec* (paprika-flavoured meat stew).

+ 197 D3 ⊠ Ulica Firingera 26 ☎ 031 369 955 ❷ Mon–Sat 9am–11pm, Sun 11–5

## SAMOBOR

### Kavana Livadić €

Samobor is known for its *samoborska kremšnita*, a delicious custard tart in layers of flaky pastry. The pastry shop attached to Hotel Livadić has the feel of a 19th-century Viennese salon, lifted with a modern boutique style.

+ 194 B3 ⊠ Trg Kralja Tomislava 1 ☎ 01 3365 850 ❷ Daily 8am–11pm

### Samoborska Pivnica €€

This beer cellar is just off the main square, behind Hotel Livadić. Low, whitewashed arches give it a cavern-like appearance. Dishes include salami or beef tongue.

+ 194 B3 ⊠ Šmidhenova 3 ☎ 01 336 1623 ❷ Daily 9am–11pm

## VARAŽDIN

### Zalogajček €

Situated in an attractive courtyard just off Varaždin's main square, Zalogajček is a great vegetarian café and delicatessen, offering tasty and inexpensive salads and a range of lunchtime specials.

+ 194 D5 ⊠ Franjevački Trg 1 ☎ 042 200 944 ❷ Mon–Fri 10–5, Sat 10–3

### Zlatna Guška €€€

Set in a cellar beneath the 17th-century Zakmardy Palace, with pikestaffs and the coats of arms on the walls, the "Golden Goose" recreates the atmosphere of a medieval castle. Dishes include the Daggers of the Count of Brandenburg (skewers of pork, chicken, beef and strawberries).

+ 194 C5 ⊠ Habdelićeva 4 ☎ 042 213 393 ❷ Mon–Sat 10am–11pm

## ZAGORJE

### Grešna Gorica €

This farmhouse restaurant has long wooden benches, tree trunks for tables and beautiful views across the hills to Veliki Tabor. Dishes such as venison goulash or roast pork are accompanied by home-made wine and followed by *štrukli* (cottage cheese strudel). There is also a small children's playground and a few farm animals.

+ 194 B4 ⊠ Taborgradska 3, Desinić ☎ 049 343 001 ❷ Daily 10–10

# Where to...
## Shop

### SAMOBOR

The two culinary specialities of Samobor are *bermet*, a herb-flavoured vermouth, and *mustarda*, a spicy mustard, both introduced by French troops in 1808. You can buy them at the **Filipec family shop**, just off the main square behind Hotel Livadić. **Ivančić**, in Plešivica, is a good place to buy local wine.

### VARAŽDIN

The pedestrianized town centre is great for shopping, especially **Gundulićeva**, with shops selling wine, leather, shoes, fashions and souvenirs. If you're after a silk tie, there is a branch of **Croata** on the corner of Trg Kralja Tomislava.

### VUKOVAR

A miniature ceramic reproduction of the Vučedol Dove (▶ 58) makes an unusual souvenir, and since the 1990s war has become a symbol of peace. You can buy one at the visitor office in the Kopački Rit Nature Park. In Ilok, **Iločki Podrumi**, on the main street, produces and sells some of Croatia's best white wines.

### ZAGORJE

A speciality of the Zagorje region is the *licitarsko srce*, a gingerbread heart decorated with icing which are traditionally given as love tokens. You can buy them in the main square of Marija Bistrica.

# Where to...
## Be Entertained

### SAMOBOR

There are parades of floats on the weekend before Lent, when people wear masks and fancy dress. The climax of the festivities is a Shrove Tuesday fireworks display.

### VARAŽDIN

The streets of Varaždin come alive each summer with artists, musicians and costumed entertainers. On Saturday mornings at 11am from May to September you can see the **Changing of the Guard** outside the town hall. In June, a **History Festival** takes place, with drama, music, dance and medieval jousting tournaments. The two-week **Špancirfest** (Street-walkers Festival; late Aug to early Sep) features open-air concerts, acrobats and pageants. During the **Varaždin Baroque Evenings** (late Sep to early Oct), classical recitals are held in the churches and theatres.

### FOLK FESTIVALS

**Brodsko Kolo**, held in Slavonski Brod in mid-June, features open-air music, dancing and a beauty contest for the prettiest woman in folk costume. **Dakovački Vezovi** (Đakovo Embroidery), in Đakovo, usually during the first weekend in July, is another big event, with *tamburica* (Slavonian mandolin) music, Lipizzaner horses and traditional wedding wagons.

# Istria and Beyond

# Getting Your Bearings

Istria (Istra in Croatian) is the most cosmopolitan region of Croatia. This northern Adriatic peninsula, virtually unaffected by the wars which destroyed so much of the country during the break-up of Yugoslavia, is now a prosperous, self-confident region and a holiday playground for millions of Europeans each summer.

Cut off from the rest of Croatia by the Ćićarija mountain ridge, Istria has always been a place apart. It was previously ruled by the Venetian and Austro-Hungarian empires, then became part of Italy between the two world wars. The Italian legacy lives on in bilingual street signs and alternative names for towns (Pula/Pola, Poreč/Parenzo, Rovinj/Rovigno, Motovun/Montona). Ports such as Rovinj, with its Venetian campanile, have a distinctly Italian feel, and the cuisine betrays an Italian influence, with pasta, olive oil and the region's truffles all used widely. The Italian city of Trieste is less than an hour away and Venice is a short trip by catamaran.

Not surprisingly, given its proximity to central Europe, Istria is where tourism has made the greatest impact. Coastal towns such as Poreč, Rovinj and Pula reverberate with Italian and German accents and there is a real buzz on summer evenings as people stroll along the promenades. Just inland is a different Istria, of vineyards, olive groves, oak woods and hilltop towns. To the south, Kvarner bay separates Istria from Dalmatia, with Croatia's two largest islands, Krk and Cres, sheltering beneath the Gorski Kotar and Velebit mountains.

Brinje

Otočac

Page 89: Impressive roman amphitheatre in the town of Pula
Right: A cobbled street in Rovinj is the perfect location for an art gallery

# In Three Days

If you're not quite sure where to begin your travels, this itinerary
recommends a practical and enjoyable three-day tour of the best of
both coastal and inland Istria, using the Getting Your Bearings map
on the previous page. The roads are good and distances
are short, so you should have plenty of time for relaxing as
well as sightseeing.

## Day 1

**Morning**
Take a walk around
the old town of
Poreč and admire
the beautiful
mosaics and
frescoes (left)
in the **❶ Basilica
of Euphrasius**
(➤ 94–95).

**Lunch**
Follow the coast
road south from
Poreč to Vrsar
and head inland
along the shores of
the Limski Kanal
(➤ 97). The village
of Flengi has several
roadside restaurants
specializing in
spit-roast pork.
Alternatively, beyond the small hamlet of Kloštar, a side road leads down
to the fiord, where a couple of restaurants sell local oysters and mussels.

**Afternoon and Evening**
Return to the coast at **❷ Rovinj** (➤ 96–98) and explore the old town. Climb
to the Church of St Euphemia to watch the sun set before enjoying a drink
at one of the waterside bars. Take your pick of the restaurants (top right)
and finish off with an ice-cream on the promenade.

## Day 2

**Morning**
Make an early start to drive down to Fažana, the starting point for the boat
trip to the **❸ Nacionalni Park Brijuni** (➤ 99–100). You can spend several
hours exploring Veli Brijun on foot, by bicycle and on the miniature road
train which tours the safari park.

**Afternoon and Evening**
Returning to Fažana,
make the short trip to
Vodnjan and have coffee
in the main square of this
charming provincial town.
If you have time, check
out the "mummies" in
the parish church. Spend
the night at **Stancija
Negričani** (➤ 108),
a beautifully converted
farmhouse just
outside Vodnjan.

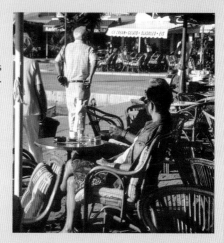

# Day 3

**Morning**
Head into **4 Pula** (➤ 101–102) to visit the Roman amphitheatre (below),
then climb to the hilltop fortress for wonderful views, before relaxing with a
drink on the old Roman forum.

**Afternoon**
Take the fast road
from Pula to Pazin
to begin a tour of
**5 Istria's hilltop
towns** (➤ 103). The
restaurants around
Buzet and Motovun
specialize in truffle
dishes, so save your
appetite for a hearty
late lunch.

**Evening**
Watch the sun set
from the church
terrace in the nearby
hill town of **Grožnjan**
(➤ 103), then have
a drink beneath
the arches of the
Venetian loggia.
Afterwards, return to
Motovun for dinner
– the town is much
quieter once all the
day-trippers have left
and is a peaceful and
atmospheric place to
stay the night.

# ◧ Basilica of Euphrasius, Poreč

**Hidden away in the back streets of Poreč, Croatia's busiest holiday resort, is this 6th-century Christian church, richly decorated with some of the finest mosaics in Europe.**

The early signs of Poreč are not promising. Between the 1960s and 1980s, it led the way in Croatian tourism and the town is almost completely engulfed by the tourist complexes of Lanterna, to the north, and Plava Laguna and Zelena Laguna to the south. The Poreč Riviera has enough beds to accommodate 100,000 visitors.

Somehow, in the middle of all this, the old town survives intact, on a fortified peninsula where the Romans built their settlement of Parentium. The original Roman grid plan has been retained, right down to the names of the intersecting north–south and east–west main streets, Cardo Maximus and Decumanus. Not far from the junction of these two streets is a magnificent example of early Christian architecture, designated a World Heritage site by UNESCO in 1997.

**View down the beautifully decorated nave of the Euphrasius Basilica, Porec**

## Visiting the Basilica

You enter the basilica complex through the atrium, a delightful arcaded courtyard. On your left is the **octagonal baptistery**, with a deep font in the middle; this also serves as the entrance to the 16th-century **bell tower**, which you can climb for views over the rooftops.

On the right as you enter the courtyard is the undoubted highlight of the complex, the **basilica church** itself. It was built between ad 535 and 550 by Bishop Euphrasius, on the site of an earlier church dedicated to St Maurus, a 3rd-century martyr and the first bishop of Poreč. Some of the floor mosaics from the original church are preserved beneath the nave and can be seen through gaps in the floor.

The long central **nave**, with its Greek marble columns and arches, leads the eye towards the apse, richly adorned with Byzantine mosaics encrusted with gold leaf and mother-of-pearl. The upper panel depicts Christ, the Light of the World, with his apostles on either side. Beneath this is a triumphal arch with the Lamb of God at the centre. The shell of the apse features a Virgin and Child, surrounded by saints and angels. To her right is St Maurus, and beyond him, a portrait of Bishop Euphrasius holding a model of his church. Completing the effect is the 13th-century **canopy** above the altar, supported by four marble pillars and decorated beautiful with mosaics.

### TAKING A BREAK

There are numerous cafés on Decumanus and the waterside Obala Maršala Tita. A good place for lunch is **Pizzeria Nono**, near the tourist office (Zagrebačka 4; tel: 052 453 088).

---

🔢 192 A4

**Basilica**
✉ Eufrazijeva ⊙ Basilica: summer daily 8–8; winter 10–7.
Museum: 10–5 💲 Church: free. Museum and campanile: inexpensive

**Tourist Information Office**
✉ Zagrebačka 9 ☎ 052 451 293; www.to-porec.comw

## BASILICA OF EUPHRASIUS: INSIDE INFO

**Top tips** Look out for the **classical concerts** which take place inside the basilica – they are usually held on Fridays in summer.
■ In summer, you can take a water-taxi to the wooded island of **Sveti Nikola**, a lovely retreat where the first public beach in Poreč was opened in 1895.

**Hidden gem** Look carefully on the right side of the apse for the **mosaic of the Visitation**, which shows a servant furtively drawing back the curtains and listening in on Mary's conversation with her cousin Elizabeth.

**In more depth** The **bishop's palace**, entered from the atrium, contains a museum of religious art. In the garden are the remains of a 4th-century mosaic floor from the original Church of St Maurus, which featured the sign of the fish, a popular symbol of the early underground church.

# 2 Rovinj

Rovinj, with its brightly coloured houses reflected in the water, huddled onto a steep-sided peninsula crowned by a Venetian-style church, is the most attractive town in Istria and one of the prettiest spots on the entire Croatian coast.

More than any other place in Istria, Rovinj manages to preserve a balance between being a historic town, a fishing port and a modern tourist resort. It is also a working town; the 19th-century cigarette factory on the quayside is the largest in Croatia and the scent of tobacco hangs in the air. This is the most Italian place in Croatia, with a sizeable Italian-speaking population.

**The seaside town of Rovinj is one of the most charming spots on the coast**

## The Old Town
The oldest part of Rovinj was built on an island, which was only joined to the mainland in 1763. The obvious approach is from **Trg Maršala Tita**, the large open square in front of the harbour. A baroque 17th-century palace off the square is home to the **Rovinj Heritage Museum**, with archaeological displays, a gallery of old masters and contemporary art exhibitions. To get to the museum, walk through the **Balbi Arch** just off the square, which was erected in 1680 and crowned by the winged lion of St Mark, the symbol of Venice.

Walk through the arch to enter the old town, a warren of narrow, steep, cobbled streets with hidden courtyards. In recent years, Rovinj has become something of an artists' colony and the main street, **Grisia**, is lined with art galleries and artists selling their work – particularly on the second

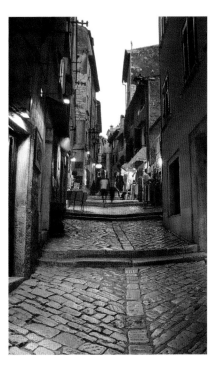

Sunday in August, when an open-air competition is held. The streets to either side of Grisia, with washing hanging from balconies, are highly atmospheric.

## The Church

Whichever route you take, you will eventually arrive at the baroque **Church of St Euphemia**, which dominates the old town. The **bell tower**, over 60m (195 feet) tall, was built in 1677 and modelled on the campanile of St Mark's in Venice. The rest of the church was built in the 18th century, though the facade is a 19th-century addition.

The church is dedicated to St Euphemia, a 3rd-century Christian from Asia Minor who was martyred during the reign of Diocletian and her body thrown to the lions. Five centuries after her death, the marble sarcophagus containing her body is said to have disappeared from Constantinople and washed up in Rovinj in AD 800. Since that time, the people of Rovinj have treated Euphemia as their patron saint and celebrate her feast day on 16 September.

**Get lost in the cobbled streets of Rovinj, lined with art shops**

The sarcophagus lies in an aisle to the right of the main altar, and a copper statue of St Euphemia alongside the wheel on which she was tortured acts as a weather-vane atop the bell tower. You can climb the 200 steep and rickety steps inside the tower for fantastic, panoramic views of Rovinj.

### Beaches and Islands

Locals gather in summer on the rocks beneath the church, where there are several concrete platforms for sunbathing. A better option is to follow the coastal promenade south from the marina into **Zlatni Rt forest park**, laid out by Baron Hütterodt between 1890 and 1910.

### LIMSKI KANAL

The west coast of Istria is cut in two by the **Limski Kanal**, a 10km (6-mile) fiord situated dramatically between thickly wooded slopes and limestone cliffs. **Boat tours** of the Limski Kanal are offered on the quaysides of Poreč, Vrsar and Rovinj in summer, and usually include a visit to a cave once used by pirates and hermits.

From the cape, there are good views to **Crveni Otok** (Red Island), the largest of Rovinj's islands, which is actually two islets connected by a causeway. The bigger island is home to Hotel Istra (➤ 109), while the smaller one is virtually undeveloped and has several naturist beaches. Boats to Crveni Otok depart regularly in summer from the main town harbour and the Delfin jetty by the marina. There are also boats to **Sveti Katarina**, an island just offshore from Rovinj.

Enjoy an evening meal in one of the restaurants in the old town at Rovinj

### TAKING A BREAK

Take your pick of the many cafés and restaurants around the waterfront. **Baccus**, just off the main square at Via Carrera 5, has Istrian wines by the glass and sells truffles and olive oil.

✚ 192 B4

**Museum**
✉ Trg Maršala Tita 11 ☎ 052 816 720 🕐 Summer Tue–Sun 10–1, 6–10; winter Tue–Sat 10–1 💰 Inexpensive

**Tourist Information Office**
✉ Obala Pina Budicina 12 ☎ 052 811 566; www.tzgrovinj.hr

### ROVINJ: INSIDE INFO

**Top tip** Watch the sunset from the church terrace or from Valentino (Ulica Svetog Križa 28), a trendy cocktail bar with cushions on the rocks, positioned so that you can almost dip your toes into the sea.

**Hidden gem** The Ruđer Bošković Institute's Centre for Marine Research, opposite the large parking area on the north side of town, houses **one of Europe's oldest aquariums**, founded in 1891, with puffer fish, scorpion fish and other local marine life (open Easter–Oct daily 9–9).

# 3 Nacionalni Park Brijuni

Roman emperors, Austrian princes and Communist heads of state have all enjoyed relaxing on these islands, which offer a superb blend of scenic beauty and historical interest, just off the Istrian coast.

The Brijuni National Park is an **archipelago** of 14 islands, 3km (2 miles) offshore from the fishing port of Fažana. Only the two largest islands, **Veli Brijun** and **Mali Brijun**, can be visited. Two thousand years ago, Veli Brijun was a summer residence for wealthy Romans; the remains of a 1st-century Roman villa can be seen in Verige Bay. Among other sights are a **Byzantine fortress** on the west coast and a 15th-century **Venetian church** containing frescoes and inscriptions in Glagolitic script (➤ 173).

**Bird's-eye view of Brijuni National Park**

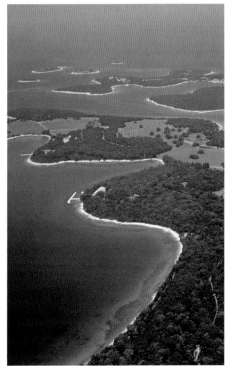

## The Modern History

In 1893 the islands were bought by Austrian industrialist Paul Kupelwieser. He employed the Nobel prize-winning bacteriologist Robert Koch to rid the islands of malaria, then he created a resort for European fashionable society. The Austrian archduke Franz Ferdinand and the author Thomas Mann were among the guests to visit Brijuni and enjoy its hotels, casino, polo club, golf course and heated sea-water pool.

In 1947, Marshal Tito chose **Brijuni** as his summer retreat and for the rest of his life he spent up to six months of the year here, entertaining world leaders from Fidel

Castro of Cuba to Queen Elizabeth II of Britain. In all, some 90 heads of state visited Brijuni, including President Nehru of India and President Nasser of Egypt, who signed the founding pact of the Non-Aligned Movement here in 1956. Since Tito's death, the islands have continued to be used by Croatian leaders. It was here in 1995 that President Tudman held a controversial meeting with his generals on the eve of Operation Storm, which liberated Croatia from Serbian forces.

## Trips and Tours

You can visit **Veli Brijun** on a national park boat trip from Fažana, which run three to four times daily in summer and once or twice daily in winter; advance booking is essential. In summer, there are also organized excursions from Pula and Rovinj. The cost includes a three-hour guided tour by miniature train, crossing open parkland with fallow deer on your way to the safari park, which contains descendants of animals donated by world leaders to Tito.

**Princess Caroline of Monaco and her daughter Alexandra, on a visit to the Brijuni Islands**

The tour also includes a visit to the **natural history museum**. Upstairs, the Tito on Brijuni exhibition has photos of Tito with his many visitors, relaxing in his orchards and wine cellar, and hunting in his private game reserve. Tito's official residence, the Bijela Vila (White Villa), can be glimpsed behind high hedges and walls on the west coast, still protected by security guards.

### TAKING A BREAK

There is a café near the harbour at **Veli Brijun**, and restaurants in various hotels.

✚ 192 B3

**National Park Boat Trips**
✉ Brijunska 10, Fažana ☎ 052 525 882; www.brijuni.hr 💰 Expensive

---

### NACIONALNI PARK BRIJUNI: INSIDE INFO

**Top tips** Guests staying at the hotels on Veli Brijun can rent bicycles and electric golf buggies to explore the island on their own, or even take a ride in Tito's 1953 Cadillac.
■ There is also a daily excursion from Fažana in summer to **Mali Brijun**, which includes a visit to an Austro-Hungarian fortress, swimming and a picnic.

# 4 Pula

The largest town in Istria is an appealing mix of bustling port city, sprawling holiday resort and historic Roman settlement, dominated by a magnificently preserved roman amphitheatre.

**The Roman amphitheatre at Pula is made from Istrian limestone**

In the 19th century, Pula was the chief naval base of the Habsburg empire and it remains a significant port today, with cranes and container ships in the harbour. Now it has become a busy tourist resort, though as most of the big hotels are to the south of the city on the Punta Verudela peninsula, the old town has survived virtually intact.

## The Arena

Begun around 30 BC during the reign of Emperor Augustus and completed during the 1st century, this is the sixth-largest **Roman amphitheatre** in the world. It was built of Istrian limestone and given an elliptical shape, some 130m (425 feet) across and 100m (330 feet) wide, with two rows of arches and an upper floor of rectangular windows set into the outer wall. In its time, it held 20,000 spectators for gladiatorial contests, and the arena is still used today for major concerts.

During the 16th century, there were plans to transport the arena stone by stone to Venice for reconstruction, but fortunately it has survived *in situ*. Most people will be content just to stand inside the arena experiencing the scale of it all, but to explore in greater depth, take the audio-tour and visit the cellars, where there is a museum of old wine and olive presses.

## Other Roman Sights

A short circuit of the pedestrianized part of town will lead you to two other interesting sights.

■ The **Temple of Augustus** was finished in AD 14 and dedicated to the first Roman emperor. The temple, with its tall Corinthian columns, stands on the edge of the old Roman forum or main square. During the summer, its collection of Roman sculpture is open to visitors. The forum is still the central meeting place of Pula, and the cafés around the square make excellent vantage points for the promenade concerts held here in summer.

■ The **Arch of Sergi**, also known as Zlatna Vrata (Golden Gate), is a triumphal arch erected by a wealthy family in the 1st century BC to honour three brothers who had fought in the battle of Actium.

**The Arch of Sergi towers over the streets of Pula**

### TAKING A BREAK

**Cvajner** Caffe (Forum 2) occupies a prime spot on the main square. Take a table out of doors or go inside for the comfy sofas, modern art gallery and beautiful 16th-century frescoes.

✠ 192 B3

**Tourist Information Office**
✉ Forum 3 ☎ 052 212 987;
www.pulainfo.hr

**Arena**
✉ Ulica Flavijevska ☎ 052 219 028
🕐 May–Sep daily 8am–9pm; Oct–Apr
9–4 💰 Moderate

**Temple of Augustus**
✉ Forum 🕐 May–Sep Mon–Fri 9–8,
Sat–Sun 10–3 💰 Inexpensive

---

## PULA: INSIDE INFO

**Top tips** The big showpiece events take place in the Roman arena, but look out for **jazz and classical concerts** in summer in the courtyard of the castle or in the small Roman theatre behind the Archaeological Museum.

■ Climb to the **Venetian kaštel**, a star-shaped fortress at the summit of the old town. The museum is uninspiring, but it is worth the entry for the views from the ramparts and the old watchtower (summer daily 8–9, winter 9–5).

■ The **Archaeological Museum** contains Roman mosaics and sculpture, as well as coins, pottery and oil lamps (summer Mon–Sat 9–8, Sun 10–3, winter Mon–Fri 9–2).

**Hidden gem** Secreted behind the parking area close to the Forum is a perfectly preserved **2nd-century Roman floor mosaic** featuring the legend of the punishment of Dirce, with the children of Zeus tying their stepmother to the horns of a bull.

# At Your Leisure

The fortified town of Buzet is the largest of the hill towns of Istria

## 5 Hill Towns of Inland Istria

Inland Istria, with its olive groves, vineyards, rolling green hills and fortified hilltop towns, is often compared to the Italian region of Tuscany. Much of the Italian population left after Istria became part of Yugoslavia in 1945, and the hill towns were largely deserted until their reinvention as alternative cultural centres.

The most visited of all is **Motovun**, perched 277m (906 feet) above the **Mirna valley** and surrounded by oak forests and vineyards producing Malvazija and Teran wines. In summer, it is so popular that the authorities levy a toll on cars; if you don't want to pay, you can park at the foot of the hill and walk up.

You enter Motovun through the **old town gate**, whose walls are lined with Roman inscriptions and Venetian stone lions; turn left beside the town loggia to arrive at the elongated main square, dominated by its 13th-century campanile. Note the old well in the square, and the relief of the winged lion of St Mark, dating from 1322.

From here you can make a brief circuit of the **medieval ramparts**, offering superb views. In recent years, Motovun has become increasingly fashionable, especially during the annual film festival in late July. Another town which has been given a new lease of life is **Grožnjan**, which was virtually abandoned in the 1960s until it was declared a "town of artists" and old stone cottages were rented out to painters and musicians. The cobbled streets and squares are great for strolling, with **art galleries** and an **international summer school** of young musicians bringing life and atmosphere to the town.

The largest of the hill towns, high above the River Mirna, is **Buzet**; from here it is a short trip to **Glagolitic Alley** (► 173) and the miniature hill town of **Hum**. In autumn you may see farmers with dogs searching for truffles in the oak woods around both towns.

➕ 192 B4

**Tourist Information Office**
✉ Trg Andrea Antico 1, Motovun
☎ 052 681 642

View across the small harbour in the town on Opatija

## 6 Labin

This medieval hill town above the east Istrian coast makes a delightful place to while away a couple of hours, with a laid-back atmosphere, art galleries and studios, and Renaissance and baroque palaces lining the cobbled streets. From the main square, **Titov Trg**, pass through the town gate and climb the steps to reach the **Church of the Virgin Mary**, notable for the Venetian winged lion on the facade.

The nearby **Lazzarini Palace** houses the **Labin National Museum** (summer Mon–Fri 10–1, 5–7, Sat and Sun 10–1; reduced hours in winter, Mon–Sat 10–1), whose most interesting exhibit, a reconstruction of a coal mine, celebrates the town's mining history. Be prepared to don a hard hat and stoop through underground passages. Afterwards, you can walk around the town walls for views to **Rabac**, a small fishing village 4km (2.5 miles) below **Labin**, where pebble coves and beaches attract visitors.

**⊞ 192 B4**

Tourist Information Office
✉ Aldo Negri 20 ☎ 052 855 560

## 7 Opatija

Opatija is the sort of place for which the words "faded elegance" were invented. Sheltered by the peak **Učka** from the cold *bora* wind, its unique microclimate on the shores of **Kvarner bay** made it the preferred winter resort of the Habsburg aristocracy, whose *belle époque* villas and hotels still stand on the seafront today, harbouring the ghosts of an earlier age. Royals, dukes and playwrights such as Anton Chekhov (1860–1904) all stayed here; the dancer Isadora Duncan (1877–1927) was inspired to create her most famous movement by the fluttering of a tree outside her window.

The finest remnant of the Habsburg era is **Villa Angiolina**, set in its own park alongside the Kvarner hotel (► 108). A 12km (7.5 mile) seafront promenade, the **Lungomare** (officially Šetalište Franz Josef I), connects **Opatija** with **Volosko north and Lovran south**, and makes

---

**FOR KIDS**

- There are **aquariums** at Pula (inside an Austro-Hungarian fortress on Punta Verudela), Poreč (just off Decumanus in the old town) and Rovinj (➤ 98).
- Mini Croatia, just outside Rovinj, has **miniature models** of buildings from all over Croatia.
- Rent **bicycles** to cycle into Zlatni Rt forest park in Rovinj (➤ 97).
- The **Roman arena** at Pula (➤ 101).
- A **cruise** on the Limski Kanal (➤ 97).

---

an equally enchanting walk by day or night, with palm and cypress trees, lush gardens, rocky coves and old-fashioned lamps.

➕ 192 C4

**Tourist Information Office**

✉ Maršala Tita 101 ☎ 051 271 310

## ❽ Rijeka

Croatia's biggest port is a busy working city, whose crumbling Habsburg-era buildings on the waterfront, with their mustard and ochre facades, include the headquarters of the Jadrolinija ferry company, adorned with reliefs and sculptures on nautical themes.

Just behind the harbour, the Korzo is the main shopping street and focus of street life. An arch beneath the clock tower leads to the oldest part of town, where you will find the round Church of St Vitus, as seen on the 100-kuna note. Climb the long flight of steps from the Rječina River or take bus No 1 to the pilgrimage church of Trsat, where angels are said to have delivered the house of the Virgin Mary in 1291. There are good views over the Rječima gorge from the nearby Trsat Castle (summer daily 9–8; winter 9–5), restored in the 19th century as a romantic folly.

➕ 192 C4

**Tourist Information Office**

✉ Korzo 33 ☎ 051 335 882

## ❾ Nacionalni Park Risnjak

When the heat of the coast gets too much, escape to this national park inland from Rijeka, with its cool beech and fir forests among the mountains of Gorski Kotar. Bears, wolves and lynx inhabit these forests, though you are unlikely to see any of them. The park office is in the village of Crni Lug; from here you can follow the Leska Trail, a well-marked 4km (2.5 mile) circuit which gives a gentle introduction to the landscapes of this region. A tougher hike leads to the summit of Veliki Risnjak (1,528m/ 5,013 feet).

➕ 193 D5

✉ Crni Lug

☎ 051 836 133; www.risnjak.hr

🏛 Moderate

**Take a stroll down the Leska trail in the Risnjak National Park**

# Further Afield

**Island of Kvarner Bay as seen from mainland Croatia**

## 🔟 Islands of Kvarner Bay

The wide **Kvarner gulf** separates Istria to the north from the Dalmatian coast to the south. Although not as attractive as some of the islands further south, those in Kvarner bay offer Roman and Venetian history, pretty harbourside towns and some of Croatia's best beaches. Each of the three main islands can be reached by ferry or bridge from the mainland, but can also be combined on an **island-hopping tour**, with ferrie that link Krk to Cres and Rab in summer.

**Eurasian Griffon Vultures at the Caput Insulae eco-centre, on the island of Cres**

## Cres

This long, narrow island, 65km (40 miles) from north to south, is actually a continuation of the partially submerged **Učka mountain range**. It is reached by regular ferries from **Brestova** in Istria and from **Valbiska** on Krk. The northern part of the island is forested and green, while the south is increasingly rocky and used mainly for sheep pastures.

On the north coast, at Beli, is the **Caput Insulae eco-centre** (summer daily 9–8, winter 9–7; closed Dec and Jan; www.caput-insulae.com), housed in an old school. Among its projects is a hospital for injured **Eurasian griffon vultures**, who breed on Cres, but whose future is threatened by the decline in sheep-farming.

The capital of the island, Cres, sits in a pretty bay sheltered by green hills and makes a pleasant place to stroll, with its Venetian loggia, clock tower, town gates and Renaissance palaces. **Osor**, on the south coast, is the oldest settlement on the island and today it has the character of an open-air museum, with its stone houses, cobbled streets and 15th-century cathedral. From Osor, a swing bridge connects Cres to the nearby island of Lošinj.

## Krk

Croatia's largest island is reached by a toll bridge at **Kraljevica**, on the coast road south of Rijeka. With its easy access to central Europe, and Rijeka airport located here, **Krk** is a popular tourist destination. The northwest coast is dominated by package-holiday resorts at **Omišalj, Njivice** and **Malinska**.

The capital, Krk, was the old **Roman city of Curicum**; traces of the Roman walls survive, along with a Romanesque cathedral and the 12th-century Church of St Quirinus, their shared bell tower topped by a distinctive onion dome. **Baška**, at the southern tip of the island, has a 2km (1.2-mile) stretch of sand and pebble beach, with views of the **Velebit mountain range** across the water. The beach gets crowded in summer, but you can always take a water-taxi to one of the nearby bays. Just inland from Baška, in the church at Jurandvor, is a copy of the Baška Tablet, an 11th-century stone containing the earliest known example of the Glagolitic script (➤ 173). The original example is kept in Zagreb.

## Rab

In summer you can take a ferry directly from **Baška** to **Lopar** on Rab, the most attractive of the Kvarner islands. The east coast, facing the mainland, is harsh and barren, battered by the *bora* wind, but the west coast is green and dotted with sheltered bays and coves. There are sandy beaches at **Lopar, San Marino** and **Kampor**, but the real highlight of the island is **Rab Town**, set on a peninsula beside its harbour. Open squares on the waterfront lead into the old town, a warren of narrow lanes intersected by three parallel streets – **Donja Ulica** (Lower Street), **Srednja Ulica** (Middle Street) and **Gornja Ulica** (Upper Street). The distinctive feature of Rab, seen from the water, is the row of bell towers

silhouetted against the skyline; you can see them all from the only remaining section of the medieval walls. You can also climb the tallest of the campaniles for views over the rooftops.

There is good swimming from the seafront promenade beneath **Komrčar Park**, or you can take a taxi-boat to **Kandarola** on the Frkanj peninsula, a naturist beach popularized by the British king Edward VIII (➤ 12–13). Ferries run to Rab throughout the year from Jablanac, 100km (62 miles) south of Rijeka.

### Cres
✚ 192 C3
**Tourist Information Office**
✉ Cons 10, Cres town ☎ 051 571 535

### Krk
✚ 192 C4
**Tourist Information Office**
✉ Trg Sveti Kvirina 1, Krk ☎ 051 221 359

### Rab
✚ 193 D3
**Tourist Information Office**
✉ Trg Municipium Arba 8, Rab ☎ 051 771 111

**Bell towers and rooftops in Rab Town**

# Where to... Stay

## Prices

Expect to pay per person per night for a double room in summer:
€ under 250kn    €€ 250kn–500kn    €€€ over 500kn

## BRIJUNI ISLANDS

### Neptun-Istra €€

Although it no longer has the cachet it enjoyed in the early 20th century, Veli Brijun still attracts the rich and famous. This smart hotel by the quayside has many rooms and suites with fabulous harbour views. The price includes unlimited boat trips to and from the mainland. You can rent bicycles, boats and horses, and discounts at the nearby golf course are available for hotel guests.

+ 192 B3 ⊠ Veli Brijun
☎ 052 525 807; www.brijuni.hr

## INLAND ISTRIA

### Kaštel €€

Set in an 18th-century town house on the main square of Motovun, Kaštel manages to combine tradition with modern style. All the rooms are brightly decorated and there is an art gallery, a peaceful garden and a pool. From the rooftop terrace views reach across the ramparts to the Mirna Valley. The restaurant specializes in truffle dishes.

+ 192 B4 ⊠ Trg Andrea Antico 7,
Motovun ☎ 052 681 607;
www.hotel-kastel-motovun.hr

### Stancija Negričani €€

Mario and Mirjana Modrušan welcome visitors to their old stone farmhouse, reached off a minor road between Vodnjan and Barban. The house has ten rooms, all decorated individually with antiques. There is a swimming pool in the gardens, as well as volleyball, bowling and swings for the children. Bicycles are available and horseback-riding can be arranged. Dinner is prepared using fresh organic produce.

+ 192 B4 ⊠ Off the road from Vodnjan to
Barban ☎ 052 391 084;
www.stancijanegricani.com

## OPATIJA

### Kvarner €€

The grande dame of Opatija hotels may have lost a little of its sparkle since it opened its doors in 1884, but it is still the only place to stay if you want to capture the faded elegance of this Habsburg-era resort. The cream-coloured neo-classical facade adorned with trumpeting angels harks back to a bygone age, and the flower-filled gardens tumble down to the sea. In the Crystal Ballroom, tea and cakes are now served beneath elegant chandeliers. Dances are still held on the seafront terrace in summer, and facilities include heated pools.

+ 192 C4 ⊠ Ulica Tomašića 1–4
☎ 051 271 233; www.liburnia.hr

### Mozart €€€

Relive the atmosphere of *belle époque* Opatija at this stylish boutique hotel, with its striking pink facade, art nouveau lobby and 26 rooms, most with balconies overlooking the sea. Despite being fitted with all modern comforts, the five-star hotel consciously imitates the Habsburg era, with staff in period costume, a Viennese-style coffee house, a pianist playing Mozart and rooms decorated in Austro-Hungarian style.

+ 192 C4 ⊠ Maršala Tita 138
☎ 051 718 260; www.hotel-mozart.hr

## POREČ

### Fortuna €€

This large modern hotel on the wooded island of Sveti Nikola is a 5-minute boat ride from Poreč on the hotel's hourly shuttle boats. It faces towards the harbour in Poreč and most rooms have balconies with sea views. Among the facilities are outdoor pools, tennis courts, watersports, a rocky beach, children's playground and nightly entertainment. The hotel also rents out apartments in Isabella Castle, a 19th-century villa on the island. Cars cannot be taken to the island, but there is a secure parking area near the harbour.

➕ 192 A4 ☒ Otok Sveti Nikola ☎ 052 465 000; www.valamar.hr ⊙ Apr–Oct

## PULA

### Scaletta €€

The charming, small family-run Scaletta is much the best place to stay in central Pula, just along the road from the Roman arena. There are only 12 quietly stylish rooms in this old town house, all decorated in warm pastel shades, with private bathrooms and air-conditioning; reservations are essential. The restaurant that is attached to Scaletta is one of the best in the whole of Pula.

➕ 192 B3 ☒ Ulica Flavijevska 26 ☎ 052 541 025; www.hotel-scaletta.com

## ROVINJ

### Adriatic €€

The oldest hotel in Rovinj, opened in 1912, has a prime position on the waterfront in a corner of Trg Maršala Tita main square. It is worth paying extra for a room with a sea view, looking out beyond the harbour to the island of Sveti Katarina. The rooms are comfortable and spacious, and the hotel has retained some of its original Austro-Hungarian charm, particularly in its Viennese-style café. It's a good place to stay if you want to be at the heart of the action, with the restaurants and bars of the seafront promenade only a few steps away.

➕ 192 B4 ☒ Obala Pina Budicina ☎ 052 815 088; www.maistra.hr

### Istra €€

Although it is something of an eyesore on the beautiful island of Crveni Otok, this large modern hotel is a good place to stay if you want a relaxing beach holiday within easy reach of Rovinj. The 352 rooms, including some family rooms, are simply furnished but comfortable. There is swimming from the rocky shore and several naturist beaches on a nearby islet, reached across a causeway. You can rent a canoe or motorboat, go windsurfing, swim in the pool, play tennis, take your kids to the playground, or eat in various restaurants and bars. And whenever you tire of the island, you can hop on the shuttle boat to Rovinj, which operates hourly throughout the summer until midnight.

➕ 192 B4 ☒ Crveni Otok ☎ 052 802 500; www.maistra.hr ⊙ Apr–Oct

### Villa Angelo d'Oro €€

Rovinj's first boutique hotel is set in a restored 17th-century bishops palace in the heart of the old town. All the rooms are individually and tastefully decorated with antiques and oil paintings, making it the ideal place for a luxurious romantic break. In summer, breakfast is served in a garden to the sound of tinkling fountains; in the evening, candles are lit here for pre-dinner drinks. There is a gourmet restaurant and a wine cellar offering tastings of Istrian wines, ham and cheese. From the rooftop loggia there are fine views out to sea. On top of all this, a shuttle boat can take you to offshore islands and beaches, and the hotel also has a private yacht for rent.

➕ 192 B4 ☒ Via Svalba 38–42 ☎ 052 840 502; www.angelodoro.at ⊙ Mar–Dec

# Where to...
## Eat and Drink

**Prices**

Expect to pay per person for a starter, main course, salad and house wine or water:

€ under 100kn     €€ 100kn–200kn     €€€ over 200kn

## INLAND ISTRIA

### Humska Konoba €

This tiny, rustic inn is behind the town gate at the entrance to Hum, "the world's smallest town", with its population of 23. It serves classic Istrian dishes such as *fuži* with goulash and roast lamb, *supa*, an Istrian special of red wine warmed in a jug and served with sugar, pepper, olive oil and toast and its own *biska* (mistletoe brandy).

🔁 192 B4 ⊠ Hum 2 ☎ 052 660 005
🕐 Jun–Oct daily 11–10; weekends only in winter

### Konoba Mondo €€

The arty Motovun restaurant is just outside the old town gates, and specializes in truffle dishes, ranging from a simple black truffle omelette to more elaborate offerings. This includes polenta with truffles and sheep's cheese or delicious fillet of beef with truffle sauce. Inside, it has a cosy and romantic atmosphere, with candlelit tables and whitewashed stone walls. On warm days you can eat on the terrace.

🔁 192 B4 ⊠ Ulica Barbacan 1, Motovun
☎ 052 681 791 🕐 Mar–Nov Tue–Sun
12:30–3:30, 6:30–9:30, Mon 12:30–3:30

### Stari Oštarija €€

The old village inn on the church square in Buzet reopened in 2005 as a classy restaurant, offering Istrian staples such as *maneštra* (vegetable soup), *fuži* (pasta), *ombolo* (pork fillet) and steak with truffles, as well as the local speciality *frittata* (truffle omelette) all accompanied by a selection of Istrian wines. For dessert, try *dolce istriano*, a home-made cake. The restaurant at Stari Oštarija is in a fabulous setting, in a stone-walled room jutting out over the cliffs, which has great views over the new town below.

🔁 192 B4 ⊠ Ulica Petra Flega 5, Buzet
☎ 052 694 003 🕐 Wed–Mon noon–10

### Toklarija €€€

From the outside, this looks like an old stone cottage, but it is in fact one of the most exclusive restaurants in Istria, set in a restored oil mill in a tiny hilltop hamlet above the Mirna valley. Don't bother coming to Toklarija if all you want is a quick, light snack This restaurant specializes in "slow food" and most visitors have five courses, which consist of soup, cured ham, pasta, main course and dessert. Reservations for Toklarija are essential.

🔁 192 B4 ⊠ Sovinjsko Polje 11 (off the main road from Buzet to Motovun)
☎ 052 663 031 🕐 Wed–Mon 1–10pm

### Zigante €€€

People come from Zagreb, Italy and Slovenia in autumn to visit this famous restaurant belonging to the Zigante Tartufi chain of truffle shops (▶ 112). It is in the village of Livade, near Motovun, among the oak forests of the Mirna valley, where Istria's truffles grow. Not surprisingly, truffles feature in almost every dish, with a choice of truffle-tasting menus at a range of prices. You can even have a refreshing truffle ice-cream for dessert.

🔁 192 B4 ⊠ Livade 7 ☎ 052 664 302
🕐 Daily noon–11

## Fjord €€

This is one of two restaurants near the jetty where the boat trips from Poreč and Rovinj stop, with a large open-air terrace overlooking the fiord. The main focus is on fresh fish and seafood, including mussels and oysters from the fiord, though you can also have an excellent and very reasonably priced *čevapčići* (spicy meatballs), which comes with chips, raw onions, *ajvar* (aubergine and pepper relish) and a selection of mixed vegetables.

🕀 192 B4 ⊠ Limski Kanal, near Kloštar ☎ 052 448 222 🕒 Daily 11–10

## OPATIJA

## Le Mandrać €€€

Situated at the end of the Lungomare promenade, with a terrace overlooking the fishing harbour at Volosoko, Le Mandrać takes the freshest local produce and gives it an unexpectedly creative twist. Seafood appears as sashimi or octopus gazpacho, while mussels

come in a soup with Istrian ham and lemon foam. If you want to splash out, go for the nine-course tasting menu, which comprises small portions of seasonal specialities. Opened in 2004, Le Mandrać restaurant has won awards for its original approach to Croatian cuisine.

🕀 192 C4 ⊠ Obala Frana Supila 10, Volosko ☎ 051 701 357; www.lemandrac.com 🕒 Daily noon–11

## PULA

## Valsabbion €€€

Valsabbion has been voted the best restaurant in Istria consistently and has won best restaurant in Croatia twice. It is widely credited with introducing the concept of "slow food" to Croatia, with fresh seasonal ingredients simply prepared to bring out their natural taste. If you are here, you may well wish to splash out on a six-course tasting menu – one focuses on meat dishes, the other on fish, with wines to

complement each course. The ultimate luxury is the ten-course gastronomic menu, full of little treats and exquisite desserts. There are a number of rooms upstairs in the chic spa hotel, that overlook the marina and the pebble beach in the seaside village of Pješčana Uvala.

🕀 192 B3 ⊠ Pješčana Uvala ☎ 052 218 033 🕒 Daily noon–midnight; closed Jan

## ROVINJ

## La Puntulina €€€

Perched at the tip of the old town above the popular bathing rocks, La Puntulina offers the most romantic setting in Rovinj, with a balcony overlooking the sea. By day, the terraces provide perfect platforms for sunbathing; at night, they turn into a fashionable wine bar where people gather to watch the sunset. The emphasis is on creative Istrian and Italian cuisine, such as carpaccio of sea bass or sole with truffles. There is also a

four-course tasting menu on offer at La Puntulina, with fresh seafood and pasta.

🕀 192 B4 ⊠ Ulica Svetog Križa 38 ☎ 052 813 186 🕒 Mar–Nov Thu–Tue, 11–3, 6–11

## Veli Jože €€

This old-style *konoba* (tavern) on the waterfront is a cut above most of the tourist-oriented restaurants around the harbour. The interior is all faux rustic, with wooden benches and walls covered in old farm tools, musical instruments and even a bicycle. In summer there are communal tables out of doors at the top of the harbour steps. The menu offers authentic Istrian cuisine – cured ham, sheeps cheese, grilled vegetables, pasta dishes, *fuži* (pasta) with goulash, roast lamb with potatoes and an excellent steak with truffles. This place is deservedly popular, so go early or be prepared to wait in order to get one of the outdoor tables.

🕀 192 B4 ⊠ Ulica Svetog Križa 1 ☎ 052 816 337 🕒 Mar–Dec daily 11am–1am

# Where to...
# Shop

Local farmer Giancarlo Zigante earned himself a place in the *Guinness Book of World Records* when he found the world's biggest white truffle, weighing 1.31kg (2.9 lb), near Buje in 1999.

His fame spread throughout Istria and he is now the owner of a chain of shops, **Zigante Tartufi**, specializing in all things tuberiferous. In addition to fresh black and white truffles, the shops sell a wide range of truffle-based products, such as minced truffles, truffle oil, truffles with olives, truffles with mushrooms, *tartufata* (truffle paste) and sheep's cheese flavoured with truffles. The staff can offer advice, recipes and can gift wrap your own selection.

Zigante Tartufi shops also sell other Istrian food and drink products such as honey, wine and *biska* (mistletoe brandy). The main shop is in Buzet, beneath the entrance to the old town at Trg Fontana (open daily 9–8; tel: 052 663 340). There are more shops at Buje, Grožnjan, Livade, Motovun and Pula, or you can buy online at www.zigantetartufi.com.

Alongside the Grožnjan shop is a wine bar, set into an old Venetian loggia where you can sample local wines and truffle-based snacks. The Livade shop also has a restaurant attached (▶ 110).

Istrian wines, spirits and Zigante Tartufi products are available from **Eva** (Ulica Veli Jože 4, Motovun) and **Baccus** (Via Carrera 5, Rovinj).

# Where to...
# Be Entertained

**Summer evenings on the Istrian coast are so delightful that for most people the entertainment consists simply of being out of doors, joining the *korzo* (evening walk) and enjoying the atmosphere at the open-air cafés.**

## MUSIC

During the summer months, look out for concerts in the churches and squares of Poreč, Rovinj and Pula. In Poreč, classical concerts are held in the Basilica of Euphrasius; in Rovinj, in the Church of St Euphemia and the Franciscan monastery; and in Pula, in the magnificent setting of the Roman arena. Recitals also take place in summer in other coastal towns such as Umag, Novigrad and Vrsar, and jazz concerts are held in the town museum courtyard in Poreč.

In inland Istria, the hill town of Grožnjan plays host each summer to **Jeunesses Musicales Croatia**, an international summer school of young musicians. You can ask at any tourist office for details of what's on locally, or keep an eye out for posters in the street.

## FILM FESTIVALS

Pula and Motovun both host international film festivals in July, with a mix of Croatian, foreign and avant-garde films. Ask at tourist offices or check out www.pulafilmfestival.hr and www.motovunfilmfestival.com.

# North and Central Dalmatia

# Getting Your Bearings

Dalmatia appears on the map as a long, thin coastal strip
between the Adriatic and the Dinaric Alps. This is where
you will find some of the most familiar images of Croatia
– harbour towns dominated by Venetian-style campaniles,
lavender-scented islands fringed by impossibly blue seas. The
northern islands around Zadar are some of the most
unspoiled in the Adriatic,
while further south,
around Split, islands
such as Brač and
especially Hvar
are growing
increasingly
fashionable
with visitors.

Velebitski kanal
Gospić
Udbir
Al
Pag
Maunski kanal
50
E65
Nacionalni Park
Paklenica
Olib
Maun
Silba
Pohlipski kanal
Silbanski kanal
Vir
Premuda
Ist
54
Molat
Sestrunj
**6 Nin**
E65
56
Zadarski kanal
**Zadar**
**7**
502
Ugljan
Al
Be
Iž
**Vransko**
Dugi Otok
Telašćica
Pašman
**Jezero**
Bay
Biograd
**8**
Žut
E6

**Page 113:**
**Clock at**
**Narodni Trg in**
**the city**
**of Split**

**Nacionalni Park 9** Kornat Murt
**Kornati**

Historically, Dalmatia has always
been separate from Croatia and
the region bears the hallmarks of its
conquerors. The Greeks established trading
colonies at Hvar (Pharos) and Vis (Issa),
introducing vineyards still in use today. The Romans
built a city at Salona; the emperor Diocletian was born
here and later retired to Split, where his palace forms the
nucleus of the modern city. The Venetians ruled Dalmatia for
almost 400 years, leaving behind beautiful churches and theatres at
Šibenik, Trogir and Hvar. More recently, northern Dalmatia became a
battleground during the war of 1991–5, when Serbian troops established
the Republic of the Serbian Krajina at Knin, cutting off Dalmatia from
the rest of Croatia. The villages inland from Zadar and Šibenik were largely
abandoned during the war and still have a ghostly feel about them today.
  Touring in Dalmatia is relatively easy. Most of the main sights are on the
Magistrala coastal highway, while regular car and passenger ferries connect
each of the islands to the mainland.

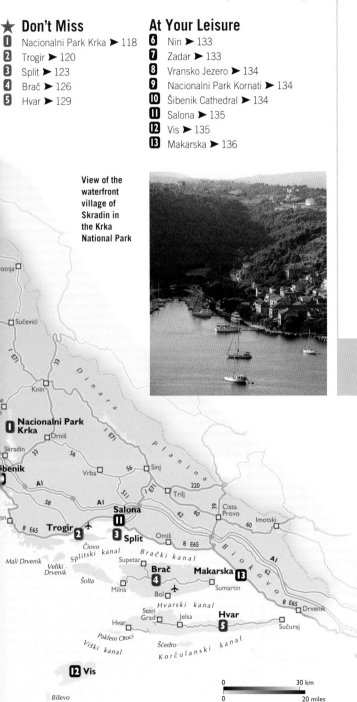

View of the waterfront village of Skradin in the Krka National Park

# In Four Days

If you're not quite sure where to begin your travels, this itinerary recommends a practical and enjoyable four-day tour of North and Central Dalmatia, using the Getting Your Bearings map on the previous page. From stunning natural scenery to laid-back island beaches, Dalmatia has it all. The islands of Brač and Hvar are very popular in summer, so expect long waits for the ferries and arrive in plenty of time.

## Day 1

**Morning**
Make an early start to explore **1 Nacionalni Park Krka** (➤ 118–119), walking around the waterfalls and taking the boat trip upriver to the monastery at Visovac and lunch at Roški Slap.

**Afternoon and Evening**
Drive down to **10 Šibenik** (➤ 134) to visit the cathedral, then take the coast road to the medieval town of **2 Trogir** (➤ 120–122). Enjoy a sunset drink at one of the cafés on the Riva, then stroll around the old town before dinner.

## Day 2

**Morning**
Don't leave Trogir without seeing the cathedral, with its magnificent carved Romanesque portal. Afterwards, you can make the short journey by car or local bus to **3 Split** (below ➤ 123–125).

## Afternoon and Evening
Take your time admiring the ruins of Diocletian's Palace, then stroll around the harbour and climb to the Marjan peninsula for woodland walks and sea views. Pause on the way down at Caffe Vidilica, whose terrace offers panoramic views over the city. Later, you can observe the evening *korzo* from a waterfront bar on the Riva. After dinner at Kod Jože (➤ 139), it is a short walk to the bus station for the ride back to Trogir.

# Day 3

## Morning
Return to Split and head down to the harbour to catch the ferry to Supetar on ◢ Brač (➤ 126–128). From here, you can make a scenic tour of the island on your way to the south coast. Take the road through the pine woods to the summit of Vidova Gora for views over Brač and Hvar. If you are feeling hungry, there is a restaurant at the summit.

## Afternoon and Evening
Continue to Bol and walk along the promenade to Zlatni Rat for a lazy afternoon on the beach (above). A 4km (2.5-mile) clifftop path leads to Murvica, where you will find Konoba Marija, one of Dalmatia's most spectacularly sited restaurants (➤ 138).

# Day 4

## Morning
In summer, take a taxi or excursion boat from Bol to Jelsa on ◢ Hvar (➤ 129–132), where you can pick up a bus to Hvar town. Otherwise the best way of getting between the islands is to return to Split and take the ferry to Hvar town or Stari Grad. If you want to drive, you must go to Stari Grad; cars are not allowed to disembark at Hvar town.

## Afternoon and Evening
Spend the rest of the day soaking up the atmosphere of Hvar town, climbing to its citadel and relaxing on its beaches. If you can, take in a performance at the Hvarsko Narodno Kazalište (Hvar Theatre, ➤ 140), one of the oldest in Europe.

# ◻ Nacionalni Park Krka

If you make only one trip away from the Dalmatian coast, it should be to the Krka National Park. Here, you can swim beneath cascading waterfalls and take a boat trip through a limestone canyon to visit a remote island monastery.

The Krka River runs for 72km (45 miles) from its source in the foothills of the Dinaric mountains near Knin to its mouth at Šibenik. For much of its length, it flows through narrow gorges, forming waterfalls and lakes rivalling those at Plitvice (► 70–72) for their beauty.

You can visit the park by bus from **Šibenik**, or on an organized excursion from one of the coastal resorts. The classic approach is from the waterfront village of Skradin, where national park boats (included in the entry fee) ferry you into the park along a wooded gorge. The boats arrive near a wooden footbridge beneath the falls at **Skradinski Buk**, the most dramatic sight in the park, which drop 45m (147 feet) in a series of 17 steps. In summer, you are allowed to swim in the shallow pool at the base of the falls. From here, an easy two-hour circuit leads on foot around the cascades.

The alternative entrance is via **Lozovac**, where there is a large parking area and shuttle buses ferrying visitors to the

Secluded island monastery on Lake Viscovac

top of the falls. This is a spectacular journey, with superb views over the river. It is still possible to make the two-hour walking circuit of the falls. From November to February, when the boats and buses do not operate, you can drive to the top of the falls from Lozovac or take your car to the foot of the falls from Skradin.

## Boat Trips

A kiosk near the shuttle bus terminus sells tickets in summer for additional boat trips along the **Krka canyon**. The shortest journey (2 hours return) is to Visovac, a Franciscan monastery founded on a rocky islet in the river in 1445. The museum contains an illustrated 15th-century Croatian version of *Aesop's Fables*, one of only three such books in the world (the others are in Oxford and Venice). Some of the

**Take a refreshing dip in the Skradinski Buk waterfalls**

boat trips (4 hours) continue to Roški Slap, a second set of waterfalls with a height of 25m (82 feet).

### TAKING A BREAK

There are cafés at Roški Slap and Skradinski Buk, both at the top and bottom of the falls. **Kristijan**, in an old stone mill above the jetty at Roški Slap, serves excellent cured ham, cheese and olives and also sells home-made wine and brandy.

🔲 198 C3 ☒ 12km (7.5 miles) north of Šibenik ☎ 022 201 777; www.npkrka.hr ⏱ Summer daily 8–8; winter 9–4 💰 Expensive (varies from 25kn in winter to 80kn in summer)

---

### NACIONALNI PARK KRKA: INSIDE INFO

**In more depth** You can take a second boat trip upstream from Roški Slap to the **Krka Orthodox monastery**, cruising through a dramatic canyon in the less visited northern reaches of the park. It may be possible to combine this with the excursion to **Roški Slap** (allow 6 hours in total), but it will probably mean spending a second day in the park and then driving to Roški Slap to begin your journey.

# ② Trogir

Trogir is one of the gems of the Dalmatian coast. Founded by Greek settlers in the 3rd century BC on an oval-shaped island, and separated from the mainland by a narrow channel, today it is a laid-back town of cafés, yachts and car-free streets, with a beautiful cathedral at its heart.

The old town is connected to the mainland by a bridge, giving easy access to the 17th-century **Kopnena Vrata** (Land Gate), an archway topped by a statue of St John of Trogir, a 12th-century bishop by the name of Giovanni Orsini who is considered the patron saint and protector of the town.

## The Old Town

From here you enter a maze of narrow streets and cobbled lanes, full of trendy shops, restaurants and art galleries. This is a town for strolling around, looking for architectural details as you stumble across courtyards, churches and palaces. The one unmissable sight is the **cathedral**, begun in the 13th century and adorned with a Venetian Gothic campanile which was added in various stages up to the 16th century. The west portal, carved in 1240 by Master Radovan, is perhaps the finest piece of Romanesque art in Croatia – a riot of saints and angels mixed with scenes from everyday life and the seasons of the calendar, illustrated through rural activities such as the grape harvest and the annual pig slaughter. The upper archway depicts the Nativity, while the pillars to either side feature Adam and Eve standing on a pair of lions. There

**Below: Intricate carvings from the cathedral at Trogir**

**Right: Boats moored at the waterfront of Trogir**

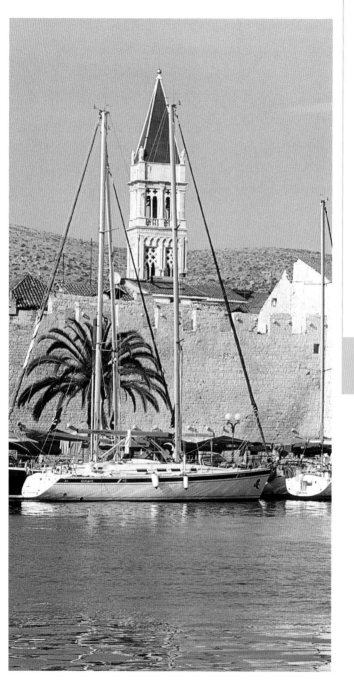

are more treasures inside the cathedral, including a 13th-century octagonal stone pulpit, carved wooden choirstalls and the 15th-century chapel of St John of Trogir, with its sculpted angels and cherubs, scallop-shell niches and elaborate carved sarcophagus.

Alongside the cathedral, the town hall displays a plaque recording Trogir's designation as a UNESCO World Heritage Site in 1997. Across the square is a Venetian loggia, once used as the town court, with a 15th-century relief of Justice by Nikola Firentinac, the architect of St John's chapel.

Gradska, the main street, leads down to the **Gradska Vrata** (Town Gate) and gives access to the **Riva**, a pleasant promenade with views across the water to the island of Čiovo. From here you can make a complete circuit of the island, passing the 15th-century Kamerlengo fortress.

Above: Town hall clock tower in Trogir

### TAKING A BREAK

There are numerous cafés and ice-cream parlours on the **Riva** and in the streets and squares around the cathedral.

🕂 199 D3

**Tourist Information Office**
✉ Gradska vrata 4  ☎ 021 881 412  🕐 Tourist Office: summer Mon–Sat 8am–8pm, Sun 8am–noon; winter Mon–Sat 8am–6pm, Sun 8am–noon. Cathedral: Jul–Aug daily 9–8; Sep–Jun 9–5  💷 Moderate

Right: View across the harbour to Split

---

### TROGIR: INSIDE INFO

**Top tips** Arriving by car, drive over the bridge to **Čiovo** and park on the far side, then walk back to Trogir, with fine views of the old town on its island as you approach.
■ Climb the tower of the **Kamerlengo fortress** (summer daily 9–7) for the best views over the town.
■ Trogir makes a good base for visiting **Split** (► 123–125), with hourly departures on bus No 37 from the bus station to the old town.
■ **Ferries** leave from the Riva in summer for the peaceful islands and bays of Veli Drvenik and Mali Drvenik.

**Hidden gem** Look above the portal of the Dominican church on the Riva to see a **carved relief of the Madonna**, accompanied by Mary Magdalene, naked apart from her hair flowing down to her feet.

# ❸ Split

Croatia's second city is built around the ruins of the Roman emperor Diocletian's palace, dating from the 3rd century. Cruise ships and ferries come and go in the harbour, the main point of departure for the Dalmatian islands.

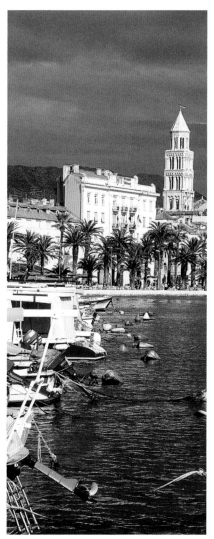

Many visitors get their first view of Split as they sail into the harbour, with the palm trees and terrace cafés of the waterfront Riva seen against a backdrop of tower blocks in the expanding modern city. This image perfectly captures the appeal of Split, a lively port city with an intriguing blend of ancient monuments and modern life. Nowhere is this more true than in the heart of the city, inside the walls of Diocletian's palace.

## Diocletian's Palace

Diocletian (AD 245–c312) was born in Salona, the son of slaves, but rose to become emperor of Rome at the age of 39. He was notorious for his persecution of Christians; among those martyred under his rule were St Maurus, bishop of Poreč (➤ 95) and St Euphemia, patron saint of Rovinj (➤ 97). An innovative ruler, Diocletian divided up the empire and introduced the concept of retirement, returning to his native Dalmatia in 305 and living out his later years in this garrison town, surrounded by the walls and towers of a splendid imperial palace which he had commissioned.

As early as the 7th century, people fleeing

### OTHER SIGHTS

■ Follow the seafront west for 30 minutes or take bus No 12 from the Riva to reach **Galerija Meštrović** (May–Sep Tue–Sun 9–9; Oct–Apr Tue–Sat 9–4, Sun 9–3), a museum and sculpture garden in the former seaside villa of the sculptor Ivan Meštrović. The ticket is also valid for the **Holy Cross Chapel**, built by Meštrović to display his *Life of Christ* cycle.

■ Climb the steps on Senjska at the west end of the Riva to reach the **Marjan peninsula**, a green hill with woodland walks, hermitage chapels and caves, and views out to sea to the islands of Šolta, Brač, Hvar and Vis. For a two-hour round walk, follow the clifftop path for 2km (1.2 miles) to the **chapel of St Hieronymus** and return via the summit at Telegrin (178m/584 feet). On the way down, stop at Caffe Vidilica, whose terrace has views over the city and port.

Salona took refuge in the palace, and it has provided a home for local families ever since. These days little of the original remains and a lot of imagination is needed to make out the shape of the original Roman palace.

Diocletian's palace is lined with cafés and restaurants

### Palace Architecture

You enter from the Riva through the **Bronze Gate**, which gives access to the Podrum or underground chambers (summer Mon–Sat 9–9, Sun 9–6; winter Mon–Sat 9–2). This is the best surviving part of the original palace and it gives a good idea of the ground plan, as these rooms stood directly beneath the imperial quarters above.

From the gallery you can climb the steps to the **Peristyle**, the central courtyard of the palace and main square of the palace complex. The black granite sphinx, guarding the emperor's mausoleum, dates from 1500 BC and was one of 12 sphinxes from ancient Egypt that once stood here; the rest were beheaded by Christians who saw them as symbols of the

**An example of the elaborate architectural detailing at Diocletian's palace**

pagan emperor. The octagonal mausoleum was transformed in the 7th century into a **cathedral** (Jun–Sep daily 8–7; Oct–May Mon–Sat 8–12, 4–7), now housing an extraordinary blend of Roman, Romanesque and Gothic architecture. Reliefs of chariot races can be seen around the dome, together with portraits of Diocletian and his wife. There are altars to the saints Domnius and Anastasius, both martyred by Diocletian and now honoured in his cemetery. You can climb the adjoining bell tower for views over the port and the palace complex.

A lane opposite the cathedral leads to the Roman Temple of Jupiter, now the **Baptistery**, whose 11th-century font is adorned with a relief of King Zvonimir, said to be the first European king immortalized in stone. Follow the Cardo, the main north–south axis of the palace, and leave through the Golden Gate, beyond which you will find a huge bronze sculpture by Ivan Meštrović (➤ 52–53). It depicts Grgur Ninski (Gregory of Nin), a 9th-century bishop who campaigned for the use of Croatian and Glagolitic scripts to replace Latin in churches. There are copies of the statue in Varaždin and in Nin itself, but this is the original.

## TAKING A BREAK

The **waterfront cafés** on the Riva make a good place to relax at any time of day.

✚ 199 D3

**Tourist Information Office**
✉ Crkvica Svetog Roka, Peristil ☎ 021 345 606; www.visitsplit.com

---

## SPLIT: INSIDE INFO

**Top tip** The city's main **food market** stands just outside the Silver (eastern) Gate of Diocletian's palace and is a good place to buy fresh fruit, vegetables, bread and cheese.

**In more depth** The **Archaeological Museum** (Jun–Sep Mon–Sat 9–2, 4–8; Oct–May Mon–Fri 9–2, 4–8, Sat 9–2), a short walk north of central Split, is the oldest museum in Croatia. It features Greek and Roman objects, including wine jars and oil lamps from Vis, and marble figures of the Roman gods Bacchus and Diana, plus jewellery, pottery and grave goods from the Roman city of Salona (➤ 135).

# ④ Brač

The largest island off the Dalmatian coast, Brač is a place of superlatives – from the highest mountain in the Adriatic you look down on Croatia's most famous beach – and it is easily reached by ferry in under an hour from Split.

The most popular way of getting to Brač is on the regular car ferry from Split to Supetar. In summer, there are fast catamarans which make the journey direct from Split to Bol on the south coast. Ferries also run throughout the year from Makarska on the mainland to Sumartin on the eastern tip of the island. In addition, Brač is the only Dalmatian island with its own airport, with connecting flights to Zagreb in summer.

Its easy accessibility means that Brač attracts the crowds, but out of season it is a peaceful island of vineyards, orchards and fishing villages hiding in sheltered bays. The island is famous for its white limestone, which has been quarried here since Roman times and used in buildings as diverse as Diocletian's palace in Split and the White House in Washington DC. Even today, you will notice that many of the houses on Brač, built from the local stone, seem to have an extra sheen.

## Arriving in Brač

Most visitors will arrive in **Supetar**, the largest town on the island, but little more than a village with low-rise houses around the harbour. There is plenty of activity by the port when the ferries come in, but at other times this is a sleepy place, where many people from Split have their summer

**Zlanti Rat is one of the best-known and most beautiful beaches in Croatia**

homes. Most of the hotels are to the west of town, where several pebble beaches face across the water towards Split.

The main road crosses the island from north to south, with a side road leading up through the pine woods to the summit of **Vidova Gora** (778m/2,552 feet), the highest mountain on any of the Adriatic islands. The peak is marked by a white stone cross; from here there are fabulous views over Zlatni Rat beach to the islands of Hvar and Korčula. It is also possible to hike up here from Bol on a well-marked path.

## The Town of Bol

Bol nestles beneath the southern slopes of Vidova Gora and is the only town on the south coast. Throughout summer, this is where the action is, with day-trippers from Hvar flocking to its beaches and tour operators advertising boat trips, windsurfing, sailing, scuba diving and free climbing (rock climbing without ropes and equipment).

The attraction here is **Zlatni Rat** (Golden Cape or Horn), easily the most photographed beach in Croatia, on a triangular spit of fine shingle which juts 300m (985 feet) out to sea, with shady pine woods at its centre. You can get there by walking along the 2km (1.2-mile) promenade that leads to the west from the harbour at Bol. Zlatni Rat is deservedly popular and it does get extremely busy in summer; to escape the crowds, you'll have to head for the rocky coves beyond, but note that some are frequented by naturists.

## Dragon's Cave

Beyond Zlatni Rat, an unmade road leads along the clifftop, arriving after 4km (2.5 miles) in the village of **Murvica**, where you will find the Konoba Marija restaurant (➤ 138). In the hills above Murvica is the extraordinary **Zmajeva Špilja** (Dragon's Cave), where dragons and mythical creatures have been carved into the rock, probably by 16th-century monks who sheltered here before founding the hermitage at **Blaca**. To visit the cave, call the guide (tel: 091 514 9787) and he will arrange to meet you at the restaurant if he is free. It is possible to get there on your own, but you will have to make do with staring at the carvings from outside the gate. Climb the path to the top of the village and follow the red arrows east for about an hour. It's a gentle ascent at first, but is followed by a steep climb up the hillside to a ruined 18th-century monastery. From here, the Dragon's Cave is now about 200m (220 yards) to your left.

Costal view from Bol to Murvica

### TAKING A BREAK

There are plenty of cafés beside the harbour in **Bol** and on the beach at **Zlatni Rat** in summer. For lunch with a particularly good view, try **Konoba Marija** (▶ 138) or Vidova Gora (summer daily 10am–midnight; tel: 021 549 061), on the summit of Vidova Gora.

✚ 199 E2

**Tourist Information Office**
✉ Porat Bolskih Pomoraca, Bol ☎ 021 635 638

---

### BRAČ: INSIDE INFO

**Top tip** Zlatni Rat may get all the attention, but the island's only sandy beach is at **Lovrečina**, 5km (3 miles) from the village of Postira on the north coast.

**Hidden gem** The 16th-century **hermitage at Blaca** can be reached on a 12km (7.5-mile) coastal path from Zlatni Rat or a rough track leading off the road to Vidova Gora. In summer, local tour operators offer boat trips from Bol harbour to Blaca Bay, followed by a short uphill hike to the monastery.

**In more depth** For a **scenic tour of northwest Brač**, take the coast road from Supetar to Sutivan, then head inland to the pretty village of Ložišća, high above a gorge. The main road continues down to the sea at Milna, set in a sheltered bay where yachts are often moored in summer. To return to Supetar, turn left in Ložišća and follow the narrow ridge to Nerežišća, passing marble quarries on the way.

# 5 Hvar

Hvar is among the most appealing of the Adriatic islands, blessed with a mild climate and covered with vineyards and lavender fields. Its capital, Hvar town, has become the most fashionable spot on the entire Dalmatian coast.

**Picturesque sunset over Pakleni Island**

The island of Hvar is a long, thin strip with a limestone ridge running along its centre and steep cliffs tumbling down towards isolated beaches and coves. In spring and early summer, the island is a blaze of colour and the soothing scent of lavender hangs in the air and wafts on the sea breeze. Even by Croatian standards, Hvar has a pleasing climate; with more hours of sunshine than anywhere else in the Adriatic.

The closest access from the mainland is the car ferry from Drvenik to Sucuraj, though this is followed by a long drive across the island to reach Hvar town. Alternatively, you can take the ferry from Split to Stari Grad, the old capital. Other options for foot passengers are a ferry from Split directly to Hvar town, or a fast catamaran from Split to Jelsa in summer.

## Hvar Town

The best way to arrive in Hvar town is by sea, from where it appears as a jumble of brown stone houses crowded around the shores of the bay, overlooked by its old castle and medieval walls. During the summer months, the port is a hive of activity, with sleek yachts moored in the harbour, ferries disembarking passengers and taxi-boats taking sunbathers

to the offshore islands. Although it has its monuments, this
is really a town for relaxing more than anything else and the
evening *korzo* is one of the liveliest in Croatia.

Café life focuses on **Trg Svetog Stjepana**, a Venetian-style
piazza which opens out to the sea, with flagstoned paving
and a 16th-century well. The west end is dominated by the
cathedral and its four-floor campanile; notice how the number
of arched windows increases with each floor. At the seaward
end of the square, beside the inner harbour, is the **Venetian
arsenal**, built to allow entire galleys to be carried inside for
repairs. The top floor houses one of Europe's oldest public
theatres, which opened in 1612 and is still in use today,
however it is currently closed for renovation and is due to
open in 2010.

Across the square, beyond the Renaissance palaces of the
16th-century nobility, steps lead up to the **Citadel** (open daily
9am–midnight; summer 9–8pm), a Venetian fortress built in
1557. There is a small museum of amphorae and you can also
clamber down and have a look at the prison cells.

The real attraction however, is the stunning view out over
the rooftops and out to the Pakleni Islands and Vis on
the horizon.

**The cathedral
looks over the
main square in
Hvar town**

## Hvar Town Beaches

A short walk south from the ferry dock leads to a Franciscan monastery, on a headland overlooking a small pebble cove. On the far side of the harbour, the seafront promenade continues westwards for some 2km (1.2 miles), passing numerous rocky beaches and bathing platforms, popular with locals in summer.

For a lazy afternoon on the beach, a better option is to take a water-taxi to the **Pakleni Islands**, an emerald-green chain of islets just offshore from Hvar town, with pine woods and remote pebble beaches. The nearest island, **Jerolim**, is used by naturists; if you want to keep your clothes on, head for the largest island, **Sveti Kliment**.

## Stari Grad

Until the Venetians moved the capital to Hvar town in the 13th century, Stari Grad was the largest settlement on Hvar, founded by Greek settlers from Paros in the 4th century BC and named Pharos (from which Hvar is derived). Its current name, Stari Grad, simply means "old town". Although not as chic as Hvar town, this is nevertheless an attractive town, in a sheltered bay beside the island's chief ferry port.

The narrow cobbled streets behind the harbour are great for strolling, stumbling across hidden gems like the 12th-century **Chapel of St John**, with its 6th-century mosaics set into the floor. Near here is the archaeological site of Greek Pharos, where excavations are still going on.

Just back from the seafront, the **Tvrdalj Petra Hektorovića** (open summer daily 10–1, 5–8) was the summer home of the poet Petar Hektorovic (1487–1572), designed as a fortress where the townspeople could take refuge in the event of a Turkish invasion. The walled garden, with its fishpond and pomegranate trees, makes a good place to sit and contemplate the Latin inscriptions with which the poet adorned his home – such as the skull and crossbones with the reminder "Neither riches nor fame, beauty nor age can save you from death".

## Jelsa

Hvar's third town, Jelsa, is on the north coast, looking across towards Brač and the Makarska Rivijera. In summer, this is

undeniably a holiday town, with cafés on the promenade and
rocky beaches backed by pine woods and hotels.

The one real sight is the 16th-century octagonal **Chapel of
St John**, in a narrow lane behind the port. A 4km (2.5-mile)
coastal path leads to the fishing village of Vrboska, a laid-back
resort with some good beaches on the Glavica peninsula.
Water-taxis make the trip from Jelsa to Vrboska in summer,
and to the islet of Zečevo, with its naturist beaches. If you feel
like a change of scene, there are also excursion boats in the
harbour offering day-trips to the famous Zlatni Rat beach on
Brač (➤ 127).

### TAKING A BREAK

The harbourside in Hvar town seems to be one endless
promenade in summer, and most visitors spend hours just
sitting at waterfront cafés and bars watching life go by and
looking out for celebrities on their yachts. **Ulica Petra
Hektorovića**, one flight up towards the castle on the north
side of the main square, is Hvar's trendy restaurant quarter,
with a choice of three classy establishments on the same street
(➤ 138–139).

✚ 199 E2

**Tourist Information Office**
✉ Trg Svetog Stjepana   ☎ 021 741 059; www.hvar.hr

Colourful fields
of lavender
in Hvar

### HVAR: INSIDE INFO

**Top tip** There are **long waits for car ferries** to and from Hvar in summer, so plan
your journey carefully and arrive at the harbour in plenty of time.

**In more depth** The pebble **beaches and coves of the south coast** are much less
developed than those in Hvar town, Jelsa and Stari Grad. Get there by taking
the road tunnel beneath the island's highest mountain, Sveti Nikola. The 8km
(5-mile) stretch between Sveta Nedjelja and Zavala features isolated beaches
and stone villages nestling beneath steep hillsides planted with south-facing
vineyards, where much of Hvar's best wine is produced.

# At Your Leisure

## 6 Nin

Crossing the stone bridge and walking through the entrance gate of this single-street town, built on an island in the lagoon at Dalmatia's northern tip, you would never guess that this was once the ecclesiastical and royal capital of Croatia. Between the 9th and 12th centuries, seven kings were crowned here and the bishop of Nin was the most powerful religious figure in the land. One famous bishop, Gregory of Nin, was immortalized in bronze by Ivan Meštrović; the original sculpture is in Split (► 125), but a copy is on display in Nin.

The greatest treasure of Nin is the 9th-century **Church of the Holy Cross**, a simple, whitewashed, domed chapel in the form of a Greek cross, which is sometimes claimed as the world's smallest cathedral. It stands all alone in a grassy field in the middle of town, surrounded by the ruins of a **Roman temple**.

Almost as spectacular is the **Church of St Nicholas**, built on a small burial mound 1km (half a mile) out of Nin on the road to **Zadar**; also dating from the 9th century, it is topped by a **16th-century tower** added by the Venetians during their battles with the Turks. **Sabunike**, 2km (1.2 miles) north of Nin, has one of the finest sandy beaches in Croatia, with views to the island of **Pag** and the **Velebit massif** across the water.

➕ 198 B4

**Tourist Information Office**

✉ Trg Braće Radića 3 ☎ 023 265 247

## 7 Zadar

The second-largest city in Dalmatia was previously the **Byzantine and Venetian capital** and a naval power to rival Venice itself. These days, it is a strange mix of sprawling suburbs and a compact old town squeezed onto a narrow peninsula still partly enclosed by its medieval walls. Largely destroyed by Allied bombs during World War II, the old town has been heavily modernized, with the result that brutal concrete architecture and shopping arcades are found side by side with **ancient churches** and cobbled streets.

At the heart of it all is the old **Roman Forum**, whose stone was used in **St Donat's Church**, a lovely 9th-century Byzantine round church dedicated to an Irish bishop of Zadar who is said to have built it himself. Next to the church is the 12th-century **Romanesque cathedral**; you can climb the bell tower for stunning views. Also on the Forum is the church and convent of St Mary, whose treasury contains an **exhibition of religious art** entitled *Zlato i Srebro Zadra* (Gold and Silver of Zadar), with extravagant ornamental reliquaries produced by the city's gold and silversmiths and a reconstruction of an 11th-century chapel (open Mon–Sat 10–1, 6–8, Sun 10–1).

Zadar's newest attraction is the playful **Morske Orgulje** (Sea Organ), with stone steps leading into the water from the Riva promenade. People come here to watch the sunset and listen to the sounds of nature created

**FOR KIDS**

- Boat trips in the Nacionalni Park Krka (► 118–119).
- Cycling and boating at Vransko Jezero (► 134).
- The beaches of the Makarska Rivijera (► 136).

by the underwater pipes. Ferries leave from Zadar for the peaceful, unspoiled islands of **Ugljan**, **Pašman** and **Dugi Otok** (Long Island).

✚ 198 B4

**Tourist Information Office**
✉ Narodni Trg 5 ☎ 023 316 166

## 8 Vransko Jezero

Croatia's largest natural lake is 25km (15.5 miles) south of Zadar, just inland from the beach resorts of **Biograd** and **Pakoštane**. Since 1999, the entire lake has been designated a nature park, attracting more than 100 species of waterfowl in winter and a colony of purple herons to the **ornithological reserve** on its northwest shore. In summer, you can rent rowing boats to go out on the lake, or follow the 30km (18-mile) cycle trail around its shore.

✚ 198 C4

## 9 Nacionalni Park Kornati

A cruise through the Kornati Islands is unforgettable. Off the coast between Zadar and Šibenik, this is an ethereal seascape of cliffs, coves, underwater caves and rocky islets, described by the Irish playwright George Bernard Shaw (1856–1950) as having been created by the gods out of the stars and their own tears.

The Kornati National Park contains 89 islands and reefs, but the archipelago has over 140, stretching north as far as the spectacular

**Telašcića Bay** on Dugi Otok. For most of the year, the islands are uninhabited, but in summer the residents of **Murter** set up fish restaurants in the bays and rent out stone cottages and fishing boats for a "Robinson Crusoe" experience. The islands are a paradise for sailors and the best way to see them is on your own yacht, though tour operators also offer day excursions from **Murter**, **Zadar** and **Šibenik**.

✚ 198 B3

**Tourist Information Office**
✉ Ulica Butina 2, Murter ☎ 022 435 740; www.kornati.hr 🎫 Park: expensive

## 10 Šibenik Cathedral

The 15th-century Cathedral of St James, standing proud above the mouth of the **River Krka**, is perhaps the finest example of church architecture in Croatia. It is mostly the work of Juraj Dalmatinac (George the Dalmatian), a Zadar-born architect who trained in Venice; a sculpture of him by Ivan Meštrović stands on the cathedral square. After his death in 1473, the work was completed by Nikola Firentinac (Nicholas of Florence), who added the dome and the distinctive **barrel-vaulted roof**. The result is a harmonious blend of Venetian Gothic and Renaissance styles. The outer portals, sculpted by Dalmatinac, are full of florid detail. The side door, facing the town hall, is flanked by

**A yacht sails near one of the Kornati Islands**

a pair of roaring lions and statues of Adam and Eve, each with one hand on their heart and the other protecting their modesty.

Near here is Dalmatinac's playful masterpiece, the frieze of **74 stone heads** running around the exterior of the apses, depicting a fascinating cross-section of 15th-century society; they are said to be portraits of those citizens who refused to pay towards the cost of the cathedral. Inside the building, don't miss the tiny hidden **baptistery**, reached down a flight of steps to the right of the altar, with delicately carved stone angels beneath a vaulted roof.

➕ 198 C3 ✉ Trg Republike Hrvatske, Šibenik
🕐 Daily 9–7 🎟 Free

## 🔟 Salona

The most significant archaeological site in Croatia is also a highly atmospheric place, the **ruins of a Roman city** of 60,000 people surrounded by fields with the tower blocks of Split visible just below. In Roman times, this was the largest town on the coast, flourishing from the 2nd century BC up until the 5th century AD; the emperor Diocletian is thought to have been born here.

Just inside the entrance gate, the **necropolis of Manastirine** has the feel of an archaeological junk shop, with tombs and sarcophagi scattered among piles of stones. In the presbytery of a Roman basilica is the **vaulted tomb** of Domnius, the first bishop of Salona, executed in the nearby amphitheatre in AD 304 during Diocletian's persecution of Christians.

From the **Tusculum archaeological museum**, a path leads to the lower town, based around the ruins of an impressive church. You can walk along the Roman walls and into the fields to reach the well-preserved **amphitheatre**, with seating for 15,000 spectators. Many of the treasures from Salona are now on display in the Archaeological Museum at Split (➤ 125).

➕ 199 D3 ✉ 5km (3 miles) from Split

Ruins of a Roman amphitheatre at Salona

☎ 021 212 900 🚌 Bus from Split
🕐 Summer Mon–Fri 7–7, Sat 9–7, Sun 9–1;
winter Mon–Fri 9–3, Sat 9–2 🎟 Moderate

## 🔢 Vis

One of Croatia's remotest inhabited islands was closed to foreigners from World War II until 1989, when it was used by the Yugoslav army as a military base. Apart from a few fishermen and winemakers, most of the islanders left during that time, but Vis is now reaping the benefit as, spared the impact of mass tourism, it is fast developing a reputation as a fashionable resort. Expensive yachts are moored in the harbour in summer, and the island can now be reached by daily catamaran from Split in under two hours.

It was the Greeks who founded the **settlement of Issa**, on the site of present-day Vis town in the 4th century BC; the remains of an **ancient Greek cemetery** lie just back from the harbour. During the Napoleonic wars (1811–15), the island was occupied by the British, who also had a base here during World War

## CASTLES IN THE AIR

Inland from the Dalmatian coast are two historic fortresses whose fortunes mirror the region's history. In the 10th century, both were strongholds for the medieval Croatian kings, while in the 16th century, they were occupied by the Turks, becoming key strategic bases on the borders of the Venetian and Ottoman empires. The **castle at Klis** (summer Tue–Sun 9–7; winter 10–4) sits on a rocky bluff just inland from Salona; you can climb its grassy ramparts for wonderful views. The **fortress at Knin** (summer daily 7–9; winter 7–3), 56km (35 miles) inland from Šibenik, was occupied in the 1990s by troops of the Republic of the Serbian Krajina, based at Knin; the Croatian flag now flies symbolically from the battlements following its liberation in 1995 in the final act of the Homeland War.

II, when Tito briefly set up his headquarters in a cave on **Mount Hum**. Walk onto the cliffs on the west side of the harbour to reach the abandoned George III fortress, with a crudely carved Union Jack (British flag) above the door and superb views over the bay towards Hvar.

On the far side of the bay, a stroll through the suburb of **Kut** leads to a small English cemetery, with memorials to victims of the Napoleonic wars and the "comrades of Tito's liberation war". Buses from te town of Vis make the journey across the island, passing vineyards and steep terraces on the way to the attractive fishing port of **Komiža**. Boats depart from Komiža in the summer months for excursions into the **Modra Špilja** (Blue Cave), which is a natural wonder on the nearby island of Biševo.

➕ 199 D2

**Tourist Information Office**
✉ Šetalište Stare Isse 5  ☎ 021 717 017

### 🔢 Makarska

The string of pebble beaches in the shadow of the **Biokovo Massif** is known as the **Makarska Rivijera**. Former fishing villages such as Brela, Baška Voda, Tučepi and Podgora are now attractive summer resorts, while the town of **Makarska**, set in a horseshoe bay, gets very lively in high season. This is where package tourism has made the greatest impact in Dalmatia, and Makarska certainly lacks the character and charm of some of the Venetian towns on this coast, though it makes a good base for a relaxed family holiday.

Looming over the coast is the table mountain of **Biokovo**, whose summit, **Sveti Jure** (1,762m/5,781 feet), is the second highest in Croatia. Climb to Sveti Jure from Makarska for views stretching all the way to Italy on a clear day.

➕ 199 F2

**Tourist Information Office**
✉ Obala Kralja Tomislava  ☎ 021 612 002

The beaches of the Makarska Rivijera lie alongside the Biokovo Massif

# Where to...
## Stay

**Prices**
Expect to pay per person per night for a double room in summer:
€ under 250kn   €€ 250kn–500kn   €€€ over 500kn

## BRAČ

### Palaca Dešković €€€
This 15th-century palace beside the harbour at Pučišća has been converted by Countess Dešković into a luxury hotel. All 15 rooms are decorated with her own paintings.
➕ 199 E3 ☒ Pučišća ☎ 021 778 240; www.palaca-deskovic.com

## HVAR

### Riva/Palace €€€
The old-style harbourside Riva hotel has been completely renovated and was reopened in 2005 as a chic boutique hotel. The Riva is also the first hotel in Croatian to become a member of Small Luxury Hotels of the World. It is owned by the same group as the Hotel Palace, which is in the old Venetian governor's palace on the main square, incorporating the clock tower and loggia in its façade. The Palace hotel has had a similar makeover to the Riva hotel, which has created a number of tasteful rooms with neutral decor.
➕ 199 E2 ☒ Riva, Hvar town ☎ 021 750 100; www.suncanihvar.com

## NACIONALNI PARK KRKA

### Skradinski Buk €
Most people visit the waterfalls as a day trip from the coast, but to explore the national park in depth, stay at this family-run hotel, which opened in 2002 in a restored town house in the waterfront village of Skradin. The 28 rooms are simply furnished and painted in warm pastel shades, and the third-floor terrace has river views. The ferry dock for the national park shuttle boats is 300m (330 yards) away.
➕ 198 C3 ☒ Burinovac, Skradin ☎ 022 771 771; www.skradinskibuk.hr

## SPLIT

### Peristil €€€
The Peristil was the first hotel within the walls of Diocletian's Palace when it opened in 2005. The hotel is a curious blend of old and new, with modern facilities side by side with Roman arches and ancient stone walls. The Peristil is a good place to stay if you want to be at the very heart of the action.
➕ 199 E3 ☒ Poljana Kraljice Jelene 5 ☎ 021 329 070; www.hotelperistil.com

## TROGIR

### Concordia €€
This 18th-century town house near the Kamerlengo fortress is now a small hotel, with views across to the island of Čiovo. All 14 rooms has a shower, TV, air-conditioning, and there is parking for guests.
➕ 199 D3 ☒ Obala Bana Berislavića 22 ☎ 021 885 400; www.concordia-hotel.net

## VIS

### Tamaris €€
A 19th-century Habsburg villa in the heart of Vis town, that is a short walk from the ferry port. The 27 rooms have high ceilings, wood floors, and rooms overlooking the harbour have lovely views.
➕ 199 D2 ☒ Obala Sveti Jurja 30, Vis town ☎ 021 711 350; www.vis-hoteli.hr

# Where to...
# Eat and Drink

**Prices**

Expect to pay for a starter, main course, salad and house wine or water, for one:

€ under 100kn     €€ 100kn–200kn     €€€ over 200kn

## BRAČ

### Konoba Marija €€

This must have the most perfect setting of just about any restaurant in Croatia – high up on a terrace, gazing across the pine woods to the island of Hvar across the sea. You can get there by walking or cycling the 4km (2.5-mile) dirt track from Bol along the cliffs to the wine village of Murvica; it is also possible to drive here. Meat and fish are barbecued on an open grill – try the Brač lamb or the mixed grill for two, perhaps accompanied by a jug of wine from the local vineyards. A nice touch is the basket of garlic bread, toasted on the grill and brought to the table with your meal.

🚹 199 E2 ⊠ Murvica, near Bol
🕓 Apr–Sep daily 10am–midnight

### Palute €

Popular Palute is right on the waterfront in Supetar, close to the dock where the ferries arrive from Split. It serves a full range of grilled meat and fish dishes at reasonable prices. Come here for good, simple, local food – try the Brač sheep's cheese followed by grilled lamb with chips and salad. The same family owns a comfortable bed-and-breakfast a short walk from the port.

🚹 199 E3 ⊠ Porat 4, Supetar
🕓 021 631 730 🕓 Daily 10am–11pm

## HVAR

### Konoba Menego €€

Dine by candlelight or eat outside, with a wine barrel for a table, at this family-run tavern in an old stone house on the steps leading up from the harbour to the castle. Everything here is home-made or produced locally, from the Pakleni Islands wine to the Hvar goat's cheese with honey. Much of the menu consists of plates of cold meats and cheeses, so it's ideal for snacking. For pudding, try the "drunken figs", stuffed with almonds and soaked in brandy, which is said to be an ancient aphrodisiac, followed by Turkish coffee with walnut or wild orange liqueur. The Kovačević family also own a vineyard and summer restaurant on the nearby island of Sveti Kliment.

🚹 199 E2 ⊠ Groda, Hvar town 🕓 021 742
036 🕓 Apr–Oct daily noon–2, 5–11

### Luna €€

Luna is one of a quartet of trendy restaurants along the same street, just a flight of steps up from the main square. This chic trattoria features Italian and Mediterranean cuisine, from fresh pasta dishes and steak with truffles to gazpacho, salads and fish stew with potatoes and white wine. On warm evenings you can dine on the roof terrace.

🚹 199 E2 ⊠ Ulica Petra Hektorovića 5,
Hvar town 🕓 021 741 400
🕓 Apr–Oct daily noon–midnight

### Paladini €€€

This elegant restaurant is housed in a lovely 16th-century Renaissance palace, once given to the noble Paladini family as reward for service in a sea battle between the

Venetian and Turkish fleets. It offers Dalmatian cuisine, fresh fish, grilled squid and pasta dishes, served in a garden of orange and lemon trees.

🚹 199 E2 ☒ Ulica Petra Hektorovića 4, Hvar town ☎ 021 742 104
🕐 May–Dec daily noon–3, 6–midnight

### Zlatna Školjka €€€

In Hvar's trendy restaurant quarter, the "Golden Shell" advertises "slow food", using local ingredients and inventive takes on traditional dishes, such as goat's cheese in olive oil, gnocchi with almonds, beef stuffed with goat's cheese or rabbit with figs. Booking is advised, especially in the months of July and August.

🚹 199 E2 ☒ Ulica Petra Hektorovića 8, Hvar town ☎ 098 168 8797
🕐 Summer daily noon–3, 7–midnight

## SPLIT

### Kod Jože €€

Hidden away in an old stone house on a quiet lane near Strossmayerov

Park, this excellent *konoba* (tavern) serves first-class meat and fish dishes. The house special is fresh fish, including sea bass, John Dory, lobster and squid, but the menu also features breaded frogs' legs, grilled vegetables and unusual offerings such as mangold risotto. There is a good selection of steaks, including one stuffed with Dalmatian ham and cheese. You can eat outside on a shady terrace, or inside, which is decorated in traditional style, with its old wine barrels and fishing nets.

🚹 199 D3 ☒ Ulica Sredmanuška 4 ☎ 021 347 397 🕐 Mon–Fri 9am–midnight, Sat–Sun noon–midnight

## TROGIR

### Konoba Škrapa €

The back streets of Trogir offer a wide choice of restaurants, many with attractive courtyards and summer gardens, but for no-nonsense, simple Dalmatian food, it's hard to beat Škrapa. It's best to

stick to the basics here, like plates of ham or steaming bowls of *fažol* (bean stew). The atmosphere is hectic and the table decorations are eccentric, but a meal here is great fun and you won't find better value for money anywhere.

🚹 199 D3 ☒ Ulica Hrvatskih Mučenika 9 ☎ 021 885 313
🕐 Mon–Sat 11–11, Sun 4–11

## VIS

### Doručak Kod Tihane €€

The first tourist hotel in Vis, dating from 1911, reopened its doors in 2004 as a smart waterfront restaurant, whose name means "Breakfast at Tiffany's". The original art nouveau interior has been carefully restored, with chandeliers and exposed stone walls. On summer nights, you can dine on the terrace, with candlelight and dreamy views across the water adding to the romantic atmosphere. The emphasis in the restaurant is on seafood, with fish pâté, shrimp

risotto, grilled squid, sautéed mussels and grilled fresh fish featuring on the menu, best washed down with the local Vugava wine. Finish your meal with a plate of *hruštule* – delicious traditional pastries from Vis.

🚹 199 D2 ☒ Obala Sveti Jurja 5, Vis town ☎ 021 718 472 🕐 Apr–Oct daily 8am–midnight

### Villa Kaliopa €€€

During the summer months, the harbour at Vis fills up with yachts, many of whose owners dine in this exclusive and romantic restaurant, with fountains and statues in the walled garden of a 16th-century villa. The menu focuses on fresh seafood and changes according to what is available locally in the market. The waiter will recommend the best dishes of the day. If you need to ask the prices, you probably can't afford to eat here.

🚹 199 D2 ☒ Ulica Vladimira Nazora 32, Vis town ☎ 091 271 1755
🕐 Summer daily 5–midnight

# Where to...
# Shop

The best shopping areas are in the towns of Split, Šibenik, Trogir and Zadar. Hvar town has a number of fashionable boutiques. Each of the islands has its own speciality – lavender in Hvar, marble in Brač, wine in Vis.

## HVAR AND VIS

Wherever you go or Hvar in summer, you will find street stalls offering **lavender** in numerous forms – dried flowers, oil and soap.

Another unusual souvenir of Hvar is **lace** made out of the agave plant; it is produced exclusively by the Benedictine nuns in Hvar town, using a technique imported from the Canary Islands. In both Hvar and Vis, you will come across wine cellars selling the local wine. Look out for the delicious dry white Vugava and the red Viški Plavac.

## SPLIT

Most of the shopping at Split is concentrated in the busy pedestrian streets of the medieval town, set back from the waterfront. The main thoroughfare is **Marmontova**, where several trendy boutiques sell women's fashions and shoes, including reasonably priced imported Italian designer brands. The stalls in the underground galleries of **Diocletian's Palace** sell arts, crafts and cheap souvenirs.

Split's main market, **Pazar**, sells a range of items and is outside the eastern gate of the palace.

# Where to...
# Be Entertained

Entertainment on the Dalmatian islands and coast takes many forms, from windsurfing, scuba diving and river-rafting to drinking at waterfront bars.

## MUSIC AND DRAMA

There are many cultural festivals in summer, with concerts and performances in local churches and open-air venues in July and August. Look out for recitals of medieval, baroque and chamber music in **St Donat's Church** in **Zadar**, concerts in **Trogir cathedral** and in the courtyard of the **Kamerlengo fortress**. In Split, performances of opera, ballet and drama take place throughout the year at the **Hrvatsko Narodno Kazalište** (Croatian National Theatre) on Trg Gaje Bulata (tel: 021 344 399; www. hnk-split.hr), but the big event is the **Split Summer Festival** (www. splitsko-ljeto.hr). For four weeks in July and August, the peristyle of Diocletian's Palace becomes an open-air stage; the highlight is the performance of Verdi's opera *Aida*.

In Hvar town, try to take in a performance at the **Hvarsko Kazalište**, which was opened in 1612, with plush red seats and a painted ceiling. It is currently undergoing further restoration and is due to open in 2010. Performances of classical and modern drama take place throughout the summer, when there are also evening concerts in the nearby Franciscan monastery.

# Dubrovnik and South Dalmatia

# Getting Your Bearings

The southern Dalmatian coastline is dominated by
Dubrovnik, a perfectly preserved walled city described
by the English poet Lord Byron (1788–1824) as the "pearl of
the Adriatic".

While much of Dalmatia was controlled by Venice, for 450
years Dubrovnik was the powerful city-state of Ragusa, paying
notional tribute to Ottoman sultans and Hungarian kings, but
refusing to be ruled by either. During its golden
age in the 15th and 16th centuries, the city
grew rich on shipping and was known as

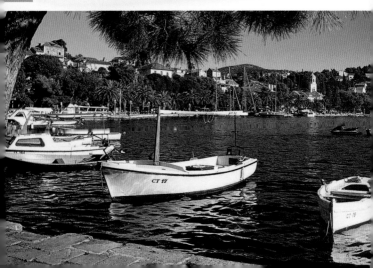

the "Croatian Athens", a melting pot of cultures and a meeting place for the greatest artists, scientists, cartographers and sailors of the day. It was during this time that the city walls were built, and a walk around the walls still provides one of the most memorable experiences of a visit to Croatia.

After suffering extensive damage during the siege of 1991–2, Dubrovnik has been brilliantly restored and once again has the feel of a lively open-air museum, with churches, palaces, cafés and flagstoned streets.

Dubrovnik makes a good base for visiting the rest of southern Dalmatia, from the unspoiled islands of Mljet, Lopud and Šipan to the vineyards of the Pelješac peninsula and the mini-Dubrovnik of Korčula town. North of Dubrovnik, the Magistrala coastal highway passes through a short section of Bosnia-Hercegovina (passports required) on its way to the Neretva delta, where many of Croatia's citrus fruits are grown. To the south, beyond the pretty resort of Cavtat, the fertile Konavle Valley is squeezed between the mountains of Bosnia and Montenegro.

**Page 141: View over the tiled rooftops of Dubrovnik**

**Left: Small fishing boats moored to the jetty at Cavtat**

**Right: The city fortifications of Dubrovnik**

# In Three Days

If you're not quite sure where to begin your travels, this itinerary recommends a practical and enjoyable three-day tour of Dubrovnik and South Dalmatia, using the Getting Your Bearings map on the previous page. Walk through woodland gardens, sample Croatia's most famous wine and visit a remote island monastery on this brief introduction to the highlights of the region.

## Day 1

### Morning
Take your time exploring
❶ **Dubrovnik Old Town** (left,
➤ 146–149), soaking up the
atmosphere in its streets and
squares. Afterwards, relax
with a coffee on the terrace of
Gradskavana before a seafood
lunch by the harbour at Lokanda
Peskarija (➤ 160).

### Afternoon and Evening
Take a stroll around Dubrovnik's
city walls, gazing down over the
rooftops and out to sea. The ticket
for the walls also gives access
to Tvrđava Lovrijenac, outside
the Pile Gate. Climb the steps to
the fortress for wonderful sunset
views, then have dinner at Orhan
(➤ 160), overlooking a peaceful
cove in the shadow of the fort.

## Day 2

### Morning and Afternoon
Go down to the harbour at Gruž to
catch the *Nona Ana* catamaran,
which leaves daily at 9am
(10am in winter) in summer for
❷ **Mljet** (right, ➤ 150–151).
This gives you six hours on the
island, enough time to explore
the Mljet National Park on foot
and by bicycle and take a boat
to St Mary's, a 12th-century
Benedictine monastery on an islet
in the middle of a lake.

### Evening
Spend your second evening in Dubrovnik inside the old city, which gets
particularly animated on summer nights. If you can, take in a performance
during the Summer Festival (➤ 162); otherwise, have dinner at Rozarij
(➤ 160–161) then head to the Troubadour café, which has live jazz at
around 10pm most nights.

# Day 3

### Morning
Head north along the Magistrala coast road, pausing to walk around the
gardens at **6 Trsteno** (➤ 156) before continuing to the **5 Pelješac**
penninsula (➤ 155–156). After a lunch of local oysters beside the
harbour at Mali Ston, you can walk off your meal with a circuit of the walls
at nearby Veli Ston.

### Afternoon and Evening
Drive across the Pelješac
peninsula, perhaps stopping
to taste and buy wine at the
Dingač vineyards in Potomje.
Arrive at Orebić in time to
make the short ferry crossing
to **3 Korčula** (right, ➤ 152–
154). Spend the evening
walking around Korčula town
and having dinner on the
sea walls at **Morski Konjic**
(➤ 161). On Monday and
Thursday nights in summer
months, you can catch a
performance of *moreška* sword
dances (➤ 26–27) beside the
Revelin tower.

# ❶ Dubrovnik Old Town

Dubrovnik is the jewel in Croatia's crown – a beautifully restored city, full of Gothic and Renaissance architecture, crowded onto a rocky headland and surrounded by its 15th-century walls.

From 1358 to 1808, this was the republic of Ragusa, one of the wealthiest cities in Europe, whose merchant fleet was reputed to be the third largest in the world. Much of the city was rebuilt following an earthquake in 1667, but although many fine buildings were destroyed, what remains has a harmonious feel.

Dubrovnik came to the world's attention during the siege of 1991–2, when Serb shells fell on the old city and over 70 per cent of houses were hit. Walking around Dubrovnik today, there are few signs of the recent war and the maps at the entrance gates, pinpointing the damage in detail, come as quite a shock. The city has recovered its confidence, the tourists have returned and there is a buzz about the outdoor cafés once again.

## Getting There

Cars are not allowed inside the walls and the old city is eminently walkable. The best entrance is through the **Vrata od Pile** (Pile Gate), where most local buses stop. Cross the stone bridge and wooden drawbridge to reach the outer gate. Above the archway is a figure of St Blaise, a 3rd-century bishop from Armenia who was martyred by the Romans and became the patron saint of Dubrovnik after he appeared in a dream to a local priest, warning of a Venetian attack. The Pile Gate leads straight into Stradun, the old city's main street. The other main entrance is the **Vrata od Ploče** (Ploče Gate), which is at the eastern end of the city, close to some of Dubrovnik's best hotels.

## Stradun

The best-known avenue in Croatia is both a busy shopping street and the venue for the *korzo* or nightly promenade. Once lined with palaces, it was rebuilt after the earthquake in a uniform style, its houses and shopfronts each have arched doorways at ground level and pretty green-shuttered window-frames above.

At the east end, beneath the clock tower, Stradun broadens out into Luja Square, with the **Orlando column** (▶ 178) in the middle. On one side is the **Church of Sv. Vlaha (St Blaise)**, with an altar containing a 15th-century gilded statue of the saint; on the other is the **Sponza** palace, Ragusa's

**Right: Rooftop view over the crowded old city**

## A WALK AROUND THE WALLS

The high point of any visit to Dubrovnik is a walk around the **city walls**, up to 25m (82 feet) high and 6m (19 feet) thick in places, reinforced with bastions and towers. The complete circuit is about 2km (1.2 miles) and takes at least an hour, looking down over courtyards, gardens and restored rooftops, as well as giving superb views out to sea and the isle of Lokrum offshore. For the finest views, climb to the roof of the Tvrđava Minčeta, designed by the Florentine Michelozzo Michelozzi in 1455. The **best place to begin** a circuit of the walls is just inside the **Pile Gate**, though there is also access from Ploče Gate and Tvrđava Sv. Ivana. The walls are open in summer daily from 9–7, in shoulder season from 9–5 and in winter months from 10–3 and the entrance fee is used to fund restoration projects. The ticket is also valid for **Fort Lovrijenac**, a free-standing fortress outside the Pile Gate.

former customs house and a rare survivor of the earthquake. It now houses the **city archives** and a **memorial room** to the defenders of Dubrovnik, who held fast during the siege of 1991–2.

### Franjevački Samostan

Just inside the Pile Gate, this **Franciscan monastery** church contains a beautiful 14th-century cloister. The museum includes a 15th-century wooden portrait of St Blaise and a painting of pre-earthquake Dubrovnik. Also off the cloister is a dispensary dating from 1317, said to be the oldest continuously operating pharmacy in Europe.

### Dominikanski Samostan

This 15th-century church is reached by a grand staircase inside the **Ploče Gate**. The highlight is the delightful cloister

The ravages of war are no longer evident in Dubrovnik old town of orange trees. The museum contains a painting of Mary Magdalene by Titian (c1488–1576), and the church features a Virgin and Child by Ivan Meštrović (1883–1962).

## Katedrala

Dubrovnik's baroque cathedral was completed in 1713, replacing an earlier church destroyed in the earthquake. The white walls give it a feeling of light and space, in contrast to the treasury behind the altar. This macabre collection features rich gold and silver filigree work, designed by local artists. Among the items on display is a skull case for the head of St Blaise, and a 16th-century casket said to contain Jesus's nappy.

## Knežev Dvor

Dubrovnik's city museum occupies the **Rector's Palace**, the former seat of the Ragusan republic where the *knez* (rector) would spend his entire term of office of just one month. The exhibits include the state apartments, which are filled with period furniture, and the former dungeons. During the **Summer Festival**, classical concerts are held out in the museum's courtyard.

---

✚ 198 B1

**Tourist Information Office**
✉ Široka 1 ☎ 020 323 587; www.tzdubrovnik.hr

**Franjevački Samostan**
✚ 202 A2 ✉ Stradun 2 🕐 Daily 9–6 💶 Moderate

**Dominikanski Samostan**
✚ 202 B2 ✉ Ulica Svetog Dominika 🕐 Daily 9–6 💶 Inexpensive

**Katedrala**
✚ 202 B1 ✉ Pred Dvorom 🕐 Summer Mon–Sat 8–8, Sun 11–8; winter Mon–Sat 8–5, Sun 11–5 💶 Treasury: inexpensive

**Knežev Dvor**
✚ 202 B1 ✉ Pred Dvorom 🕐 May–Oct daily 9–6; Nov–Apr Mon–Sat 9–2 💶 Moderate

---

## DUBROVNIK OLD TOWN: INSIDE INFO

**Top tips** The tourist office on Stradun has free copies of the **monthly Best in Dubrovnik**, with museum and event listings, bus maps and timetables.
■ Dubrovnik's **city beach** is at Banje, outside the Ploče Gate, a broad sweep of pebble beach with views to the old town.

**Hidden gem** The **Sinagoga** (Synagogue) on Ulica Žudioska serves Dubrovnik's small Jewish community, one of the earliest Sephardic congregations in the world, following their expulsion from Spain in 1492. Among the items on display in the museum is a list of earthquake victims from 1667 and a memorial to 27 Dubrovnik Jews who died during the Holocaust.

# ❷ Mljet

The southernmost of Croatia's major islands is a beautiful and unspoiled place of pine and oak forests, steep cliffs, saltwater lakes and coves.

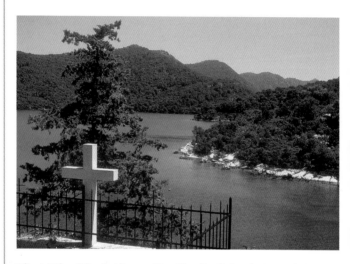

Mljet is 37km (23 miles) long and just 3km (2 miles) wide. It has a mythical appeal for Croatians, as the legendary home of the nymph Calypso, who is said to have seduced Ulysses and held him captive for seven years in her cave on the south coast after he was shipwrecked on the island. The story is told by Homer in his epic poem *Odyssey*.

**Mljet island is now a national park**

## Mljet National Park

Most people come here on day trips to visit the **Nacionalni Park Mljet**, which covers 31sq km (12 sq miles) of forest and lakes on the west of the island. The easiest way to get there is on the daily catamaran *Nona Ana*, which makes the journey from Dubrovnik in under two hours. Tickets go on sale at 8am each morning by the quayside at Gruž. From June to September, the boat takes you to **Polače**, inside the national park, allowing you six hours on the island; at other times, when the boat drops you at Sobra, you will probably need an overnight stay. In summer, you can also visit Mljet on organized excursions from Dubrovnik, Cavtat, Korčula and Orebić, with entry to the national park included in the price.

## Exploring Mljet

Arriving at **Polače**, you can buy a ticket and pick up a map from the kiosk by the harbour. The ticket includes a minibus transfer to the park headquarters at Pristanište, but it is just as pleasant to walk on the well-marked path beginning behind

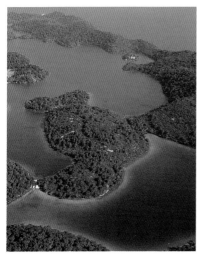

the ruins of a 4th-century Roman palace. This brings you out by the shore of Veliko Jezero, the larger of two saltwater lakes connected to the sea by a narrow channel. A footpath leads around the two lakes, which meet at Stari Most (Old Bridge), where you can rent bicycles, canoes and rowing boats in summer.

The ticket also includes a boat transfer from Pristanište or Stari Most to **St Mary's Island**, where you will find one of Croatia's most photographed sights – a 12th-century **Benedictine monastery**, on an islet in the middle of the lake. Used as a hotel during the Yugoslav era, the monastery is now in a poor state of repair, but it is still an atmospheric place.

A bird's-eye view of the island of Mljet

### TAKING A BREAK

There are several cafés and restaurants on the **seafront at Polače**, a summer restaurant on **St Mary's Island**, and another, **Mali Raj**, on the shores of Veliko Jezero.

➕ 198 A1

**Nacionalni Park Mljet**
✉ Pristanište 2 ☎ 020 744 058; www.np-mljet.hr 💷 Expensive

---

## MLJET: INSIDE INFO

**Top tip** Climb to the summit of **Montokuc** (253m/830 feet), the highest point in the national park, for views across the island. The path is signposted from the shores of Veliko Jezero, near Pristanište.

**In more depth** Although most people visit on day trips, it is possible to stay on the island. There is a **hotel at Pomena** (▶ 159), and several places offer rooms on the waterfront at Polače. Saplunara, on the southern tip of Mljet, has one of Dalmatia's finest sandy beaches; although the village is almost deserted, local families rent out rooms here and set up fish restaurants in summer.

# ❸ Korčula

The Venetian walled town of Korčula is like a miniature version of Dubrovnik, standing proud on its own peninsula, with the sea on three sides. It lies on the edge of one of the greenest islands in the Adriatic, with cypress and pine forests and vineyards, which were planted by the ancient Greeks.

The easiest way of getting to Korčula from southern Dalmatia is on the regular ferries from Orebić on the Pelješac peninsula. The car ferry arrives at **Dominće**, 2km (1.2 miles) south of Korčula town; if you are touring without a car, there is a passenger ferry which docks right on the harbour at Korčula. The main coastal ferry from Rijeka to Dubrovnik calls in at Korčula, and there are also ferries and catamarans from Split to Vela Luka, the island's main town, 45km (28 miles) from

Korčula at its western tip. A direct fast ferry service from Dubrovnik to Korčula was introduced in 2007.

## The Town

Korčula is a compact town, huddled onto a narrow peninsula and still largely enclosed by its medieval walls and round towers. The old town is perfect for walking, and the stroll around the outer walls on a pine-shaded promenade takes all of 15 minutes. From here there are views to the mountains of the Pelješac peninsula, just 2km (1.2 miles) away.

The main entry to the old town is through the **Kopnena Vrata** (Land Gate), reached by a broad flight of steps leading up to the Revelin Tower. Above the arch is a relief of the winged lion of St Mark, the symbol of Venice. The 15th-century tower has been restored to house a permanent exhibition on the *moreška* sword dancers (➤ 26–27), who can be seen performing nearby twice a week in summer.

From here, a single street runs the length of the old town, with narrow lanes dropping down to the sea on either side. Almost immediately you reach the tiny main square,

**A passenger ferry moored in the harbour at Korčula**

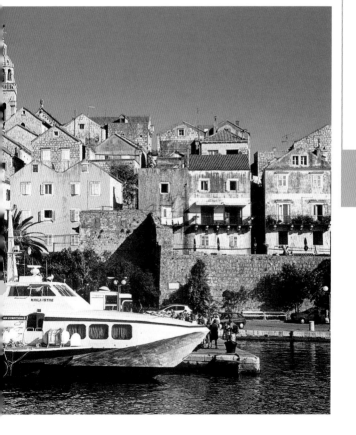

dominated by the **Cathedral of St Mark**, begun in the 13th century and completed over the next 300 years in a mix of Gothic and Renaissance styles.

The cathedral **Treasury** (open summer daily 9–2, 5–7) houses an eclectic collection of artworks, from a 15th-century altarpiece to a naive *Annunciation* by local artist Ana Fištanic. The Town Museum (open Jul–Aug daily 9–9; Apr–Jun and Sep–Oct 9–2) occupies a 16th-century palace across the square. Near here is **Marco Polo's House**, said to be the birthplace of the Venetian traveller Marco Polo (1254–1324). You can climb the tower for beautiful views in the summer; there are plans to open a Marco Polo Museum here.

**TAKING A BREAK**

The **Massimo cocktail bar** (open May–Oct daily 6pm–2am, moderate) on Šetalište Petra Kanavelica makes a great place for a sunset apéritif on the sea walls.

 199 F2
**Tourist Information Office**
✉ Obala Franje Tuđmana  ☎ 020 715 701

The Kopnena Vrata (Land Gate) is the main entrance into the Old Town

## KORČULA: INSIDE INFO

**Top tips** Try to catch a performance of the *moreška* sword dance, which takes place at festivals and on Monday and Thursday evenings throughout the summer.

■ Look out for the **white wines** produced on the island, not just Grk from Lumbarda but also Pošip and Rukatac.

■ Take a water-taxi in summer to the **island of Badija**, which has several good pebble beaches, including one naturist beach. Alternatively, take a bus or boat trip to the **wine village of Lumbarda**, 6km (4 miles) from Korčula, where you can walk through the vineyards to the beautiful sandy beach at Pržina.

**Hidden gem** The **Icon Museum** (summer daily 10–1, 6–8, shoulder months 9–2), in a narrow lane off Šetalište Petra Kanavelića, contains a collection of Cretan Orthodox icons, looted during a war between Venetian and Turkish troops. A covered bridge from the museum leads into All Saints' Church, with a carved wooden altarpiece sheltering beneath a 15th-century canopy.

# At Your Leisure

## 4 Lastovo

This remote island south of Korčula was closed to foreigners from 1976 to 1989 and is still very much off the tourist trail, though it is fast developing as an escapist destination for sailors and independent tourists. The island is linked to the mainland by a daily ferry from Split, and there are also plans to introduce a twice-weekly fast ferry service from Dubrovnik and Korčula. Ferries arrive at the port of **Ubli**, 10km (6 miles) from **Lastovo town**, the island's biggest village.

With a population of under 1,000, Lastovo feels like a place apart and there is little to do but walk in the fertile countryside, swim from secluded beaches and take boat trips in summer to the uninhabited islets of the archipelago. Like Istria, Lastovo was part of Italy between the two world wars and many older people speak Italian.

On Shrove Tuesday each year, the island plays host to one of Croatia's strangest **Carnival celebrations**, when a straw figure known as **Poklad** is paraded through town on a donkey before being ritually burned, while dancers perform a local variation of the **Korčula sword dance**.

➕ 199 F1
**Tourist Information Office**
✉ Lastovo town ☎ 020 801 018

## 5 Pelješac

This long mountainous finger of land is effectively an island, known throughout Croatia for its expensive Dingač and Postup red wines. A single road runs the 90km (56-mile) length of the peninsula, with views across to the islands of Korčula, Lastovo, Mljet, Hvar and Vis from beaches on the west coast.

The twin towns of **Mali Ston** and **Ston guard** the entrance to the peninsula, fortified by 14th-century walls which once formed the second longest defensive system in the world, after the Great Wall of China. You can walk right around the walls at Ston; the section from here to

Vineyards on the Pelješac peninsula

### PELJEŠAC WINES
You can taste and buy local wines at the **Dingač and Matuško Vina wineries** in the village of **Potomje**. The best red wine, Dingač, is produced from Plavac Mali grapes grown on the southern sea-facing slopes.
■ **Dingač** (tel: 020 742 010).
■ **Matuško Vina** (tel: 020 742 393).

Grotto in the botanical gardens at Trsteno Arboretum

Mali Ston has been recently restored. From Ston, the road passes through the vineyards at **Potomje**, the heart of production for Dingač wines, on its way to the pleasant beach resort of **Orebić**, 2km (1.2 miles) from Korčula across a narrow channel.

➕ 198 A2
**Tourist Information Office**
✉ Trg Mimbeli, Orebić ☎ 020 713 718

### ⑥ Trsteno

The 16th-century aristocrat Ivan Gučetić built his summer villa in the seaside village of Trsteno, where leading poets, artists and statesmen of Ragusan society would gather to discuss politics and stroll in the elegant gardens overlooking the sea. The house and garden remained in the Gučetić family until 1947, when they were confiscated by the state.

Now an **arboretum**, the gardens make a lovely place to walk, with shady avenues, hedges and exotic trees, many grown from seeds brought back by local sailors from their travels. The highlight is the **ornamental fishpond**, just behind the villa, where a figure of Neptune with his trident stands guard over a grotto, flanked by a pair of nymphs.

The gardens were badly damaged by fire caused by shelling in 1991, but fortunately they have recovered well. A steep path leads down to Trsteno's harbour, with views of the Elafiti Islands offshore.

➕ 198 B1 ☎ 020 751 019 ⑨ Summer daily 8–7; winter 8–5 ▦ Moderate

### ⑦ Elafitski Otoci

The tiny Elafiti ilands of **Koločep**, **Lopud** and **Šipan** provide peaceful havens just a short ferry ride away from the bustle of Dubrovnik.

**FOR KIDS**
■ The **walk** around Dubrovnik's city walls (▶ 148).
■ *MOREŠKA* sword dances on Korčula (▶ 26–27 and 154).
■ **Swimming** in the Dead Sea on Lokrum (▶ 157).
■ The **beaches** around Cavtat (▶ 157).

## ČILIPI

Cavtat is the main town of the Konavle region, a narrow strip of land between Dubrovnik and the Montenegrin border. The area is known for the **folk costumes** of its inhabitants, which can be seen every Sunday morning in summer in the village of **Čilipi**, when **folklore performances** and **traditional courtship dances** are put on for tourists in front of the church.

During the golden age of Ragusa, many Dubrovnik nobles built their summer houses here, and the islands are still a popular weekend retreat. There are regular ferries to the Elafiti Islands from the harbour at **Gruž**, with additional fast shuttle boats from Dubrovnik's old port in summer, making it possible to combine a trip to two of the islands in one day.

With orchards, vegetable gardens, vineyards, pine woods, ancient stone chapels and churches, fishing villages, quiet beaches and fewer than 1,000 permanent residents, the islands have a relaxed, laid-back charm. The best sandy beach is at **Šunj** on Lopud.

➕ 198 B1

## 🄱 Lokrum

Just 15 minutes by boat from Dubrovnik, the wooded isle of Lokrum (➤ walk on pages 180–182) makes a popular half-day outing. The English king Richard the Lionheart (1157–99) is said to have been shipwrecked here on his way back from the Crusades, while in the 19th century the island was a summer retreat for Archduke Maximilian von Habsburg, younger brother of the Austro-Hungarian emperor Franz Josef I, who converted the old **Benedictine monastery** into a private villa and laid out the formal gardens, still visited today.

There is good swimming here, both in the warm saltwater lake known as the **Mrtvo More** (Dead Sea) and from the spectacularly sited naturist beach on the east side of the island, signposted from the jetty. Boats depart regularly for Lokrum in summer from the old harbour at Dubrovnik (from 9am, last return 6pm, 40kn) in winter, there are also occasional weekend excursions, or you may find a taxi-boat which will take you.

➕ 198 B1

## 🄴 Cavtat

Cavtat is less than 20km (12 miles) south of Dubrovnik and only a few minutes from the airport. It is one of Croatia's prettiest resorts, set around a horseshoe bay enclosed by peninsulas on both sides, with views to the isle of **Supetar** and **Dubrovnik** in the distance. In the 3rd century BC, this was the Greek town of **Epidaurum**; a thousand years later, its inhabitants fled northwards to found Dubrovnik.

The painter Vlaho Bukovac (1855–1922) was born here and you can visit his house and studio near the waterfront; his image of 19th-century Cavtat harbour can be seen above the chancel in the nearby Church of Our Lady of the Snows. A path from here leads to the summit of the **Rat peninsula**, the original site of Greek Epidaurum, where you will find the domed **Račić mausoleum**, designed by Ivan Meštrović for a local shipping magnate.

With cafés on the palm-lined promenade and 5km (3 miles) of seafront paths linking beaches and pine woods, Cavtat makes a good base for a relaxing seaside holiday. There are a number of boats which depart regularly, throughout the summer months, for the old harbour in Dubrovnik.

➕ 198 C1 🚌 Bus 10 from Dubrovnik

## Tourist Information Office
✉ Tiha 3 ☎ 020 479 025

# Where to... Stay

**Prices**

Expect to pay per person per night for a double room in summer:

€ under 250kn    €€ 250kn–500kn    €€€ over 500kn

## CAVTAT

### Supetar €€

This small, attractive hotel is set in an old stone house on the waterfront, with lovely views across the bay to the Sustjepan Peninsula. It is just a short distance from a pebble beach and concrete bathing platform, though guests also have access to the swimming pool at the Hotel Croatia, a large, luxury five-star hotel belonging to the same company on the other side of the bay. Hotel Croatia is only a few minutes walk away from the cafés and restaurants of the seafront promenade, where boats depart regularly for Dubrovnik.

➕ 198 C1 ✉ Obala A. Starčevića 27 ☎ 020 479 833; www.hoteli-croatia.hr/supetar ⏱ Apr–Oct

## DUBROVNIK

There are just two small hotels inside the old city of Dubrovnik. Most of the top hotels are outside the Ploče Gate, while the majority of package accommodation is on the Lapad and Babin Kuk peninsulas, 5km (3 miles) west of the city, or in the resorts of Cavtat, Mlini and Plat to the south.

### Grand Villa Argentina €€€

The guest list at the Argentina has included Tito, Margaret Thatcher, Richard Burton and Elizabeth Taylor. The hotel, traditionally considered the top address in town, is made up of four separate villas, including the lovely 1930s Villa Orsula and the early 20th-century folly Villa Scheherazade, as well as a modern building. Steps lead down through the gardens to a small private beach; there are also outdoor seawater and heated indoor pools. The sea-facing rooms have views to the old town, a 10-minute walk away.

➕ 202 off C2 ✉ Frana Supila 14 ☎ 020 440 555; www.gva.hr

### Hilton Imperial €€€

One of Dubrovnik's earliest hotels, built in 1895 just outside the Pile Gate, reopened in 2005 under the management of the Hilton chain. The Imperial combines art nouveau architecture and charm with all the modern facilities you would expect, including an indoor pool and fitness club with saunas and Jacuzzis. The rooms have wood and marble fittings; some have balconies with sea views.

➕ 202 off A2 ✉ Ulica Marijana Blažica 2 ☎ 020 320 320; www.dubrovnik.hilton.com

### Pucić Palace €€€

This five-star boutique hotel opened in 2003 in an 18th-century palace overlooking the market square in the old town. It's a gem of a place, whose atmosphere of informal luxury set the trend for small town-house hotels in Croatia. The 19 rooms have original artworks, antique furniture, handwoven rugs and dark oak parquet floors, along with modern conveniences such as DVD players and satellite TV. Dining options include a boulevard café, wine bar and terrace restaurant (summer only) serving Middle Eastern cuisine. A private yacht is also available for guests to rent.

**➕ 202 B1 ⊠ Ulica Od Puča 1**
**☎ 020 326 200; www.thepucicpalace.com**

### Stari Grad €€€

The only other place to stay within the old town walls is this small hotel, with just eight rooms, in an old mansion close to the Pile Gate. Its old mirrors, chandeliers, antique furnishings and rugs lend it a great deal of charm. A highlight is the small roof terrace, with magnificent views over the city.

**➕ 202 A2 ⊠ Od Sigurate 4**
**☎ 020 322 244; www.hotelstarigrad.com**

### Vila Curić €€

These 14 modern self-catering apartments are in a quiet street on the Babin Kuk peninsula, overlooking Gruž harbour and the Rijeka Dubrovačka bridge. All have a kitchen, bathroom and living-room. Some have a balcony or terrace. The beaches and promenades of Babin Kuk are close by and the old city is a bus ride away, making this a good place to combine a seaside holiday with a city break.

**➕ 202 off A2 ⊠ Ulica Mostarska 2**
**☎ 020 436 555; www.vila-curic.hr 🚌 Bus 6**

### Villa Dubrovnik €€€

This low-rise white Modernist villa, hidden among fragrant gardens filled with orange and lemon trees, has long been the most romantic place to stay in Dubrovnik. Steps lead down to a private beach, and the cliffside terraces have views of Lokrum and the Old Port – just a short boat trip away on the hotel's private shuttle. Originally built as a rest home for Communist officials and used to house refugees and soldiers during the Homeland War, the hotel is showing its age. It closed in 2007 for renovation, completed in the summer of 2009.

**➕ 202 off C2 ⊠ Ulica Vlaha Bukovca 6**
**☎ 020 422 933; www.villa-dubrovnik.hr**
**🕓 Apr–Oct**

### Zagreb €€

This old-style hotel on the Lapad peninsula was first opened in 1932. The rooms are simply furnished but very comfortable, set in a handsome pink-painted 19th-century villa with tall palm trees in the garden. The pebble beach at Lapad cove is just over 100m (110 yards) away, and there are regular buses to Pile Gate.

**➕ 202 off A2 ⊠ Šetalište Kralja Zvonimira 27, Lapad ☎ 020 438 930; www.hotels-sumratin.com 🚌 Bus 5, 6, 7 🕓 Apr–Oct**

## KORČULA

### Korčula €€

The large package hotels are all on the fringes of Korčula town, but if you want to be more central and don't mind dated rooms, the best choice is the Korčula. With 20 rooms in a white stone building dating from 1912, it stands just outside the town walls, beside one of the entrances to the old town. Be sure to have an evening drink on the west-facing waterfront terrace, which is perfectly placed to catch the sunset and has views across to the Pelješac peninsula.

**➕ 199 F2 ⊠ Obala Franje Tuđmana 5, Korčula town ☎ 020 711 078;**
**www.htp-korcula.hr**

## MLJET

### Odisej €€

The only large hotel on the island is inside Mljet National Park, beside a small cove in the pretty seaside village of Pomena. The 156 rooms are spread out across a number of whitewashed pavilions, and there are also two apartments (€€€) that have their own kitchenette, living-room and balcony with sea view. This is a good base for an active holiday, with scuba diving and sailing courses on offer, and bicycles for rent. A short walk from Pomena leads through the woods to Malo Jezero, a small saltwater lake.

**➕ 198 A1 ⊠ Pomena ☎ 020 362 111;**
**www.hotelodisej.hr 🕓 Apr–Oct**

# Where to...
# Eat and Drink

## Prices

Expect to pay per person for a starter, main course, salad and house wine or water:

€ under 100kn    €€ 100kn–200kn    €€€ over 200kn

## CAVTAT

### Galija €€€

This old-style tavern and wine cellar is on a cobbled street leading uphill towards the cemetery. You can eat indoors in winter, but the main attraction on summer evenings is the beautiful seaside terrace, with tables set with candles and fine linen beneath the pine trees. The Dalmatian food and wine are first-class, from the free starter of fish pâté to smoked ham, seafood risotto, boiled sea bass, grilled fish and barbecued steaks. More inventive offerings might include sea urchins, shrimps in honey or carpaccio of grouper with parmesan and rocket (arugula), an excellent choice for a celebration meal.

**✚ 198 C1 ⊠ Vuličevićeva 1
☎ 020 478 566 ⊙ Daily 11am–midnight**

## DUBROVNIK

### Buffet Škola €

The tiny Buffet Škola, just off the Stradun, makes the best sandwiches in town. Nothing fancy, just thick slices of crusty home-made bread filled with Dalmatian ham or cheese in oil and tomato. You can find it at the foot of a narrow alley leading up towards Prijeko. In summer there are also a couple of tables out on the street for alfresco snacking.

**✚ 202 B2 ⊠ Antuninska 1
☎ 020 321 096 ⊙ Daily 8am–midnight**

### Lokanda Peskarija €€

Locals come here for good, fresh, simply cooked seafood, right beside the harbour. Choose from mussels, prawns, oysters, squid, grilled fish or seafood risotto, served with salad and dry white wine. At lunchtime be sure to arrive in plenty of time at Lokanda Peskarija, or be prepared to wait.

**✚ 202 C1 ⊠ Na Ponti ☎ 020 324 750
⊙ Daily 8am–midnight**

### Mea Culpa €

For a good-value lunch, you can't beat this popular pizzeria in the back streets of the old town. The pizzas are cooked in a wood-fired oven; other choices include lasagne and salads. There are a few tables inside, but most people eat outside on the cobbled street.

**✚ 202 A1 ⊠ Za Rokom 3 ☎ 020 323 430
⊙ Daily 8am–midnight**

### Orhan €€€

This smart fish restaurant outside the Pile Gate is one of Dubrovnik's best-kept secrets. Take the steps down to the waterfront beneath the Lovrijenac Fortress and you will find it among the upturned fishing boats, beside a peaceful cove which once served as the city's main harbour. On summer evenings, you can dine on a covered terrace right beside the sea. The house special is fresh fish, brought to your table on a tray to help you make your choice. If you don't want the fish, other options include steaks, schnitzels, risottos and pasta dishes.

**✚ 202 off A2 ⊠ Od Tabakarije 1
☎ 020 414 183 ⊙ Daily 11am–midnight**

### Rozarij €€

Tucked away in a corner at the far end of Prijeko, Rozarij is far more intimate and discreet than the rows of identical tourist restaurants along the rest of Prijeko. In summer, tables are put outside on the terrace in front of the Church of St Nicholas and along the narrow passageway leading to the Dominican monastery. The restaurant serves Dalmatian staples, such as grilled fish, steak and cuttlefish risotto, generous salads and excellent Turkish coffee.

🔢 202 B2 ☒ Prijeko 2 ☎ 020 321 257

🕙 Daily 11am–midnight

### Sesame €€

This tiny, arty bistro outside the Pile Gate is popular with students. The walls are lined with old theatre posters and programmes for the Dubrovnik Summer Festival dating back 50 years, as well as a grenade from the 1991–2 war. The restaurant operates separate lunch and dinner menus, both Mediterranean in flavour but with a handful of good pasta dishes, and unusual salads such as smoked ham

with figs or octopus with cheese. Vegetarians are well catered for – try the vegetable sorbet, courgette carpaccio and pasta with truffles.

🔢 202 off A2 ☒ Ulica Dante Alighierija

☎ 020 412 910 🕙 Daily 8am–11pm

### Adio Mare €€

A touristy but atmospheric place to eat in Korčula is this down-to-earth tavern near the cathedral, with stone walls and communal wooden tables and benches. The menu, which has hardly changed for 30 years, features Dalmatian classics like *brudet* (fish soup with polenta), *pržolica* (beef with cabbage) and *pasticada* (stewed veal with onions, tomatoes and prunes), along with steaks and kebabs, which are barbecued on live coal on an open fire in the corner. There are no reservations, so arrive early.

🔢 199 F2 ☒ Ulica Svetog Roka 2, Korčula town ☎ 020 711 253

🕙 Apr–Oct daily 6pm–midnight

### Maslina €

Set among olive groves on the road from Korčula to Lumbarda, this small family-run restaurant is renowned for its excellent home-cooked food throughout the summer months. House specials include macaroni and *pogača*, a pizza-like dish of crusty bread topped with tomatoes, onions, peppers, aubergines, courgettes, olive tapenade and melted cheese. You can also eat outside on the terrace in the summer months, but be aware that there is no sea view, because the restaurant is situated right next to the road.

🔢 199 F2 ☒ Lumbarajska Cesta

☎ 020 711 720 🕙 Summer daily 11am–midnight

### Morski Konjic €€

This long terrace restaurant takes up virtually the whole of the eastern promenade, with tables on the sea walls looking across the water to the Pelješac peninsula. The wide-ranging menu includes meat

and fish dishes such as plain grilled fish, mussels and octopus salad, washed down with the local Grk and Pošip wines.

🔢 199 F2 ☒ Šetalište Petra Kanavelića

☎ 020 711 878 🕙 Apr–Oct daily 8am–1am

### Kapetanova Kuća €€

People come from far and wide to sample the local oysters at Mali Ston, which are famed for their aphrodisiac qualities. There are several good restaurants on the picturesque waterfront but "the captain's house" is the best, offering fresh and grilled oysters, oyster soup and beef in oyster sauce, as well as local mussels, lobster and fresh fish. Mali Ston has become a very popular honeymoon destination and the owners of Kapetanova Kuća also run a small boutique hotel called Hotel Ostrea (€€).

🔢 198 B1 ☒ Mali Ston ☎ 020 754 264

🕙 Daily 9am–midnight

# Where to...
## Shop

### DUBROVNIK

The shops along Stradun are designed to appeal mainly to tourists to Dubrovnik, offering T-shirts, souvenirs, postcards, books and CDs. For a wide range of foreign-language books about Croatia, check out the branch of **Algoritam** (Stradun 8). Most of the old town bookshops sell books and videos about Dubrovnik during the siege of 1991–2.

For more unusual boutiques, you need to leave Stradun and explore the narrow streets to the south. **Od Puča** is the main shopping street of the old town, with small offbeat shops specializing in costume jewellery, clothing, antiques and modern art. Several shops at the western end of **Od Puča** sell intricate gold and silver jewellery in filigree designs, a speciality of Dubrovnik since the days of the Ragusan republic. If you're after a silk tie, a branch of **Croata** is at Pred Dvorom 2, beside the cathedral. The pharmacy in the cloisters of the **Franjevački Samostan** (Franciscan monastery; ▶ 148) sells herbal remedies dating back to 1317.

The morning market in **Poljana Gundulićeva**, at the eastern end of Od Puča, is a lively affair, with farmers selling cheeses, fruit liqueurs and fresh produce.

For Dalmatian wines and spirits, check out **Vinoteka** (Stradun) or **Dubrovačka Kuća** (Ulica Svetog Dominika), inside the Ploče Gate.

# Where to...
## Be Entertained

### CAVTAT

Look out for performances of *klapa*, male-voice choirs who perform without instruments; concerts are held outside the parish church on summer evenings.

### DUBROVNIK

During the **Dubrovnik Summer Festival** more than 80 performances of drama, opera, music and ballet take place at open-air stages in the old city. The festival starts each year with a fireworks display on 10 July and finishes on 25 August. For information contact the festival office (tel: 020 326 100; www.dubrovnik-festival.hr) or visit the kiosks at Stradun and Pile Gate.

The monthly *Best of Dubrovnik* booklet gives details of other events. During the summer months, the Lindo folk ensemble perform traditional songs and dances on Monday and Friday evenings at Lazareti, the former quarantine hospital outside the Ploče Gate. Jazz fans should head for Troubadour, a bar in Bunićeva Poljana, for live jazz at 10pm most nights in summer.

### KORČULA

The *moreška* sword dance (▶ 26–27) is performed Monday and Thursday evenings in summer beside the Land Gate and at festivals, with the biggest on 29 July. For further information and tickets contact local travel agents.

# Walks and Tours

# 1 Zagreb Old Town

*Walk*

**DISTANCE** 2.7km (1.6 miles) **TIME** 1–1.5 hours **START/END POINT** Trg Bana Jelačića ➕ 201 D3

This short walk, beginning and ending in Zagreb's central square, explores the oldest and most attractive part of the capital – the maze of narrow streets and squares known as Gornji Grad (Upper Town). A funicular tramway takes you up the hill, avoiding a steep ascent on foot. Although it is possible to complete this walk in an hour, it is best to allow half a day to enjoy the various churches and museums along the way, go shopping in Dolac market and soak up the atmosphere of this historic district.

## 1–2

Start in **Trg Bana Jelačića** (➤ 46–48) beside the statue of Governor Josip Jelačić on horseback. With your back to the statue, face half-right and head for Dubrovnik Kavana, with outdoor tables on the corner of Ulica Ljudevita Gaja (also known as **Gajeva**, ➤ 166 panel). This is the entrance to a busy pedestrianized area of shops, cafés and ice-cream parlours which is particularly animated on summer evenings. Walk down Gajeva and

turn right opposite the glass facade of the Hotel Dubrovnik into Ulica Mirka Bogovića (Bogovićeva), a busy promenade lined with

open-air cafés and bars. The street ends in **Trg Petra Preradovića**, a large square with more cafés and a cinema.

## 2–3

Turn right here, passing the statue of Petar Preradović (1818–72), a soldier and romantic poet. Just beyond the statue is the Serbian Orthodox Church, the meeting place of the city's Serbian minority, which remained remarkably untouched during the conflict with Serbia in the 1990s.

Emerging on Ilica, Zagreb's main shopping street, turn left and take the first right into Ulica Tomića (**Tomićeva**).

**The funicular connects the Upper and Lower towns**

## 3–4

Now you have a choice. The easy option is to take the funicular (*uspinjača*), which runs every 10 minutes from 6:30am to 9pm. This delightful ride, the oldest form of public coloured roof tiles of St **Mark's Church (Sv. Marka)** up ahead. Take the first left along Ulica Vranicanijeva and turn right along **Ulica Matoša (Matoševa)**, passing the Hrvatski Povijesni Muzej (Croatian History Museum) on your left.

## 5–6

At the end of this street, turn left and immediately right onto **Ulica Mesnička**, where you will see the **Prirodoslovni Muzej** (Natural History Museum), an eclectic collection housed in an old theatre, on your left. Follow this street until you reach a Classical-style archway leading to a school. Turn right here along

KAPTOL

BRANJUGOVA

Katedrala

GORNJI GRAD

Kaptol

Trg A Stepinca

JURIŠIĆEVA

Tkalčićeva

Dolac

Pod zidom

AMRUŠEVA

Stjepana Radića

Kamenita Vrata

8

7

9

Bakačeva

i

10

Opatička

Markov trg

Sabor

Trg Bana Jelačića

1

PRAŠKA

6

Sv Marka

Kam

Habdelić

Sv Katerina

Gajeva

N TESLE

Demetrova

Fondacija Ivan Meštrović

Matoševa

Katarinin Trg

4

Uspinjača

ILICA

Bogovićeva

MASARYKOVA

Prirodoslovni Muzej

5

Mesnička

Hrvatski Muzej Naivne Umjetnosti

Strossm Šetalište

Kula Lotršćak

Trg Petra Preradovića

2

Tomićeva

3

ILICA

0  200 metres

0  200 yards

transport in Zagreb, first opened in 1893 as a steam-powered railway and was electrified in 1934. With a speed of 1.5m
(5 feet) per second and a journey time of under a minute, it is sometimes said to be the shortest public transport journey in the world. Alternatively, you can climb the flight of steps beside the tramway to reach the Upper Town of Gradec.

## 4–5

Emerging from the funicular station, a leafy promenade, **Strossmayerovo Šetalište**, runs both left and right, following the route of the old city walls. Ignore this and keep straight ahead, passing to the right of the Tower of **Lotršćak** with a glimpse of the

Ulica Mletačka, passing the **Fondacija Ivan Meštrović** (➤ 52–53) on your left. Turn left at the end of the street to enter **Markov trg** (St Mark's Square).

### 6–7

This square is the symbolic heart of Croatia, lined with baroque palaces and government buildings. On one side is the **Sabor** (Croatian parliament), on the other the offices of the presidency in the former Banski Dvor (Governor's Palace). It was this building that was hit by a Serbian rocket attack in October 1991, when President Tudman was meeting here with his cabinet – an event described in detail in the **City Museum** (➤ 54).

Cross to the far side of the square for the best views of St Mark's Church, then continue walking downhill in the direction of the Tower of Lotrčšak, passing the **Hrvatski Muzej Naivne Umjetnosti** (Naïve Art Museum, ➤ 54) and Greek Orthodox Church of St Cyril and St Methodius on your right. Returning to the crossroads just before the tower, turn left to see St Catherine's Church (**Sv. Katerina**). This is the city's baroque masterpiece, with the facade featuring sculptures of the Virgin Mary and the four evangelists.

### STREET NAMES

Most streets in Zagreb have at least two different names – the one seen on street signs and the one used in conversation and on maps. Thus Ulica Gaja becomes Gajeva, Ulica Bogovića becomes Bogovićeva, Ulica Tomića becomes Tomićeva, Ulica Radica becomes Radićeva and Ulica Tkalčića becomes Tkalčićeva. To confuse matters further, the square which is the start of this walk, Trg Petra Preradovića, near the start of this walk, is universally referred to by the locals as Cvjetni Trg (Flower Square) because of the flower market that is still held there.

### 7–8

Turn left beside the church to enter Jezuitski Trg, where the former Jesuit monastery is now an art gallery hosting temporary exhibitions. At the crossroads, notice the old pharmacy on the corner of Ulica Kamenita, in business since the mid-14th century. Turn right to walk through the **Kamenita Vrata** (Stone Gate), one of the four original entrances to the walled town of

**As you walk through Zagreb, look out for details such as this wall sign in Kaptol**

**The richly decorated nave of St Catherine's Church, in the Upper Town**

home to fashionable boutiques and trendy, youthful bars. The street lies on the dried-up channel of the former stream which once separated Kaptol from Gradec.

Gradec. According to legend, after much of the old town was destroyed by fire in 1731, a painting of the Virgin Mary was discovered completely undamaged in the ashes. To celebrate this miracle, the gate was rebuilt and it now houses a shrine, full of flickering candles and devout pilgrims at prayer.

## 8–9

After passing through the gate, take the steps to the right beside the George and Dragon statue and turn right along Ulica Radića (Radićeva), a steep cobbled street lined with art galleries and souvenir shops. Turn left onto **Krvavi Most** (Bloody Bridge), the historic boundary between the townships of Kaptol and Gradec, whose name reflects the violent confrontations that used to take place between the two. Looking up, the spires of the cathedral are visible above the houses. Cross the bridge to reach **Ulica Tkalčića (Tkalčićeva)**, one of the city's most attractive promenades, whose 19th-century houses are now

## 9–10

Turn left and then right onto Ulica Skalinska to arrive on the upper level of **Dolac market**, with clothes stalls in the street to your left and farmers selling fresh produce down below. Take the steps down to the main market square and continue in the same direction towards the **katedrala** (cathedral, ▶ 50–51). When you reach the street named Kaptol, with the cathedral directly ahead of you, turn right to return to **Trg Bana Jelačića.**

### TAKING A BREAK
**Mala Kavana**, on the north side of Trg Bana Jelačića close to the equestrian statue, is an old-style café serving good coffee and cakes. For drinks, just take your pick of the trendy bars along Ulica Tkalčića (Tkalčićeva). A good place for lunch is **Kerempuh** (▶ 61), on the upper level of Dolac market.

# 2 Zagorje
*TOUR*

This scenic drive makes a circuit of the Zagorje (▶ 73–75), a bucolic region of cornfields, meadows, vineyards, pretty villages, hilltop churches and fairy-tale castles between Zagreb and the Slovenian border.

Although you could easily spend several days exploring this region, it is possible to cover the main sights in a day trip from Zagreb, adding around two hours to the total time.

---

**DISTANCE** 148km (92 miles), plus 10km (6 miles) with the diversion to Trakošćan **TIME** 3.5 hours
**START/END POINT** Marija Bistrica ✚ 194 C4

**1–2**

Start in the pilgrimage town of **Marija Bistrica** (▶ 74) and take the road to Donja Stubica. The road out of town is not well signposted, so it is easier to take the main road to Zagreb south from the church and turn right when you reach a junction on the edge of town. Stay on this gentle road as it winds through the peaceful Stubica valley beneath the northern slopes of **mount Medvednica** (▶ 59), whose TV mast is visible on the summit. The first village of any size is Gornja Stubica, known as the birthplace of a Peasant's Revolt in 1573, which is commemorated in the Muzej Seljačkih Buna (Museum of Peasant Uprisings). Shortly afterwards, you reach the lovely village of Donja Stubica, where a road beside the church square leads to the summit of Sljeme, making a spectacular drive to Zagreb.

### 2-3

Continue on this road through the spa town of Stubičke Toplice, where the road bends right, following signs to Zabok. After a further 2km (1.2 miles), turn left at a roundabout towards Zabok. The road crosses the Zagreb-Krapina motorway, bypasses Zabok and continues for 20km (12.5 miles) to **Kumrovec** (▶ 82–83), rising and then falling to the dramatic Sutla valley, right on the Slovenian border. Shortly before Kumrovec, you enter the Zelenjak Gorge, with the forested hills of Slovenia visible across the river. On your right, you pass the Lijepa Naša monument, a stone obelisk dedicated to local poet Antun Mihanović (1796–1861), the author of the Croatian national anthem (▶ 170).

### 3-4

Just after passing Kumrovec, you reach a fork in the road, where you must keep right to Miljana – a left fork would take you to a Slovenian border post instead. Note the hilltop church on the horizon, high above the thickly wooded slopes. Now you are in the

rural heart of the Zagorje, all farmsteads, barns and roadside shrines, and cottages offering *seoski turizam* (agrotourism; ▶ 16–17). The road climbs to the village of Zagorska Sela, which is dominated by the Church of Sveta Katerina, and then continues to Miljana.

### 4-5

Turn right here towards Desinić or you will soon reach another border post. Shortly you will see the castle of **Veliki Tabor**

(▶ 73) perched on a hill to your left. After exploring the castle, drive through the village of Desinić and take the left fork towards Pregrada.

### 5-6

Arriving in Pregrada, turn right along the main street, following signs to Zagreb. After 5km (3 miles), turn left beside the Dvorec Bežanec hotel and stay on this road as it rises and falls through the vineyards, before dropping steeply to Krapina (▶ 75).

**Lace-making is a regional speciality**

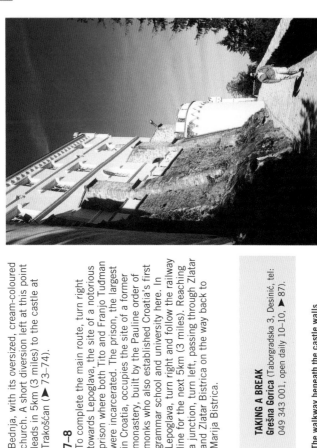

Bednja, with its oversized, cream-coloured church. A short diversion left at this point leads in 5km (3 miles) to the castle at Trakošćan (▶ 73–74).

## 7–8
To complete the main route, turn right towards Lepoglava, the site of a notorious prison where both Tito and Franjo Tuđman were incarcerated. The prison, the largest in Croatia, occupies the site of a former monastery, built by the Pauline order of monks who also established Croatia's first grammar school and university here. In Lepoglava, turn right and follow the railway line for the next 5km (3 miles). Reaching a junction, turn left, passing through Zlatar and Zlatar Bistrica on the way back to Marija Bistrica.

### THE CROATIAN NATIONAL ANTHEM
Croatia's national anthem is *Lijepa Naša Domovino* (Our Beautiful Homeland). The words were written by Antun Mihanović in 1835. It was first performed as the national anthem in 1891 and was readopted in 1990, shortly before independence from Yugoslavia.

*Our beautiful homeland,*
*O so fearless, our beloved country,*
*Our fathers' ancient glory,*
*Shall always be blessed!*

*You are our only glory,*
*You are our only treasure,*
*We love your plains and valleys,*
*We love your hills and mountains.*

## 6–7
Turn left as you enter Krapina, passing the **Muzej Evolucije Hasnjakovo** (Museum of Evolution) on your left. Continue on this road as it runs beside the railway line, then turn right, signposted to Varaždin, passing beneath the busy motorway high overhead. Stay on this minor country road to reach the village of

### TAKING A BREAK
**Grešna Gorica** (Taborgradska 3, Desinić, tel: 049 343 001, open daily 10–10, ▶ 87).

**The walkway beneath the castle walls at Trakošćan**

**DISTANCE** 68km (42 miles) **TIME** 1.5 hours **START/END POINT** Pazin ✚ 192 B4

# 3 Istrian Hill Towns
*Tour*

Although they lie just a short distance inland from the busy coastal resorts, the hill towns of Istria offer a completely different experience. Even if you are staying by the sea in Poreč, Pula or Rovinj, it is worth renting a car for the day and heading inland among the vineyards, olive groves and oak woods. This short, easy circuit takes in two of the most dramatic hill towns, though it can easily be extended to include others (▶ 103) or taken as a leisurely half-day excursion from the coast.

## 1–2

Begin in **Pazin**, which can be reached on the fast highway connecting Rijeka with Rovinj and Pula. This small industrious town of around 10,000 inhabitants may not have immediate appeal, but it repays an hour or two of exploration. The highlight is the castle, first mentioned in AD 983 as

The fortified walls of the hilltop town of Buzet

a gift of Emperor Otto II of Hungary to the bishop of Poreč. The castle, which now contains an ethnographic museum (summer Tue–Sun 10–6; reduced hours in winter), overlooks a great gorge known as Pazin's Pit, where the River Pazinčica swells after rain, almost encircling the town.

Although he never visited Pazin, the French novelist Jules Verne (1828–1905) was inspired by the pit – the hero of his novel, *Mathias Sandorf*, was imprisoned in the castle and escaped by swimming along the underground river and into the sea.

Leave Pazin by taking the main road through the middle of town in the direction of Rijeka and the Učka Tunnel. After 2km (1.2 miles), you will see a right

turn leading to the motorway to Rijeka. Ignore this and keep straight ahead, crossing fertile countryside with the peaks of Učka, often covered in snow, rising in the distance.

After 8km (5 miles), you come to the village of Cerovlje, known for it's brickworks.

**2–3**
Turn left immediately before the level crossing on the old road to Buzet, and left again at the next junction. The road now rises to Kovačići, where a panoramic view of central Istria opens out in front of you. Ahead and to the left is the Butoniga valley, with a lake in the middle and views across the plain to the hill town of Motovun in the distance; to the right is the Čičarija ridge, dividing Istria from Slovenia and the rest of Croatia.

Rijeka

Čičarija

Roč

Hum

Draguć

A8

3

2

Cerovlje

Buzet

201

4

A9

SLO

1

Pazin

★

6

Rovinj

Istarske Toplice

Motovun

Beram

5

Škropeti

Mirna

Buje

48

21 E751

0                    5 km
0              3 miles

Shortly afterwards, you reach the village of **Draguć**, little more than a single street of houses and a tall church perched on a cliff. In the 1970s and 1980s, Draguć was known as the "Istrian Hollywood" as a number of films were shot here, but these days the village is largely deserted. The 12th-century Romanesque Chapel of St Elisium and the 14th-century Church of St Rock are both renowned for their frescoes; the latter, painted by Master Anthony of Padova, features vivid images of biblical scenes including the Adoration of the Magi and the Annunciation. The churches are normally kept locked, but if you want to have a look inside, ask around in the village and you may find the keyholder, who will let you in for a small donation.

## 3–4

The road continues as far as **Buzet**, the largest of the hill towns, on a bluff 151m (495 feet) above the River Mirna and still partly enclosed by its medieval walls and gates. In recent years, Buzet has become Istria's self-styled "city of truffles" and each autumn it attracts a large number of visitors who come here to taste and buy this expensive delicacy.

## GLAGOLITIC ALLEY

A short diversion along the road from Buzet to Rijeka leads to Roč the start of the so-called "Glagolitic Alley". This 7km (4-mile) **sculpture trail** between Roč and Hum commemorates the Glagolitic script, a 41-letter **Slavonic alphabet** devised in the 9th century by the Greek brothers St Cyril and St Methodius, who were instrumental in converting Croatia to Christianity. The script was widely used in liturgical texts in Croatia between the 11th and 19th centuries, and the first known printing of a Glagolitic missal took place in Istria in 1483. There are 11 **sculptures** along the trail, which recall **significant events** and important symbols in Istrian and Croatian history. Look out for the stone featuring the Glagolitic, Latin and Cyrillic alphabets – Glagolitic was a forerunner of Cyrillic, which is named after St Cyril and is still used in Russia, Bulgaria and Serbia today. The trail ends in Hum, the self-proclaimed "smallest town in the world", with just 23 inhabitants, an annual election for mayor and a copper town gate engraved in the Glagolitic script.

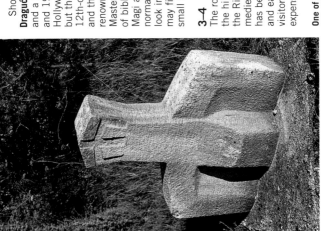

**One of the Slavonic alphabet stones along Glagolitic Alley**

## 4–5

At Buzet, turn left to follow the main road along the Mirna valley towards Buje. You pass the spa town of **Istarske Toplice**, whose waters have been known for their healing properties since Roman times. Stay on this road as it continues through the narrow valley with oak woods and tall crags to either side. When you reach a crossroads, turn left and take the bridge across the river towards **Motovun** (➤ 103), the best known and most spectacularly sited of the Istrian hill towns. After another 2km (1.2 miles), you can park at the foot of the hill and then climb up to Motovun, or pay a toll in the summer months and drive up.

## 5–6

Stay on this road and turn left at a junction to return to Pazin. Along the way you will pass the small village of **Beram**, noted for its 15th-century cycle of frescoes. They are in the chapel of the Virgin Mary, which is just outside the village, and feature a macabre Dance of the Dead, depicting not only skeletons, but a rich gallery of human characters from medieval Istria. The message behind these frescoes is, of course, that all humans are equal at the hour of death.

The town of Motovun is the best sited of all the Istrian hill towns

# 4 Dubrovnik Old Town
## Walk

**DISTANCE** 3km (2 mile) **TIME** 1 hour **START/END POINT** Vrata od Pile (Pile Gate) ✚ 202 A2

The classic walk in Dubrovnik may be the circuit of the city walls (➤ 148), but it can be just as rewarding to stroll inside the ramparts, discovering hidden lanes and courtyards in the oldest parts of the city. Even when Stradun is thronging with visitors, it is usually possible to find a quiet corner just a few streets away. This short walk explores the narrow lanes rising above Stradun to either side, so involves a fair degree of climbing. Most local buses stop outside Pile Gate, the start point for the walk; arriving by boat from Cavtat at the old harbour, you need to walk the length of Stradun to reach the start.

### 1–2

Begin just inside **Pile Gate** beside the **Onofrio Fountain**. This large domed structure, with water spouting from sculpted masks, is a popular meeting place where buskers entertain the crowds. The fountain was completed in 1444 by the Neapolitan engineer Onofrio della

Cava to supply fresh water to the city. It was badly damaged during the earthquake of 1667 and again during the siege of 1991–2, but has now been restored to some of its former glory. The nearby Church of **Sveti Spasa** (St Saviour) is used for summer evening concerts.

Walk straight ahead along **Stradun**, whose limestone paving has been polished to a sheen

#### MEDIEVAL GRAFFITI

From Ulica Od Puča, near the start of the walk, a few steps right along Ulica Zlatarica lead to one of Dubrovnik's hidden gems. Look carefully and you will see some graffiti, dated 1597, etched into the outside wall of the Church of St Rock. Translated from the Latin, it serves as a warning to children playing ball in the street: 'I'm warning you, players...peace be with you, but remember that you will die'.

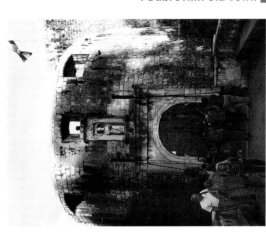

The Pile Gate entrance into the walled city

by the many footsteps passing this way over the centuries. Almost immediately, look for an archway to your right and pass beneath the arch into **Ul ca Gariste**. At the next crossroads, turn left into **Ulica Od Puča**, the main shopping street of the old town. There are several good jewellery shops here selling the distinctive local gold and silver filigree work, as well as art galleries, haberdashers and wine shops.

**2–3**
Turn right at **Ulica Široka**, passing **Dom Marina Držića**, the former home of the playwright Marin Držić (15C8–67) on your left. Držić was known for his bawdy comedies, performed in the fashionable Renaissance salons of Dubrovnik, Venice and Zagreb. The house is now a museum, with audiovisual displays giving an insight into 16th-century society. Continue straight ahead and climb the steps beside the Domino steak house, then turn right along Ulica Od Rupa. A short distance along on your left is the **Etnografski Muzej Rupe**, an ethnographic museum in the former city granary, with deep storage pits carved out of the rock. The terrace in front of the museum has fine views over the city, sheltering beneath the bulk of Mount Srđ.

**3–4**
Turn left alongside the museum to ascend the narrow staircase of **Ulica Od Šorte**. As you climb, notice the protruding stone struts on the fronts of the houses, with pierced holes through which washing lines would be suspended for drying laundry or woollen yarn (Dubrovnik was known for its textiles in medieval times). At the top of the street, turn left to walk beside the former Benedictine convent of St Mary. After being ransacked and dissolved by Napoleonic troops during the French occupation (1805–15), the convent became a barracks and later a military hospital, and is now an apartment block. The entrance to the main courtyard features a relief of the Annunciation beneath the coats of arms of Dubrovnik and noble families.

Stay on this cobbled path through one of the oldest and highest districts of the city until you come to some peaceful garden allotments beneath the city walls. The path now drops steeply beside the walls and a gap in the wall to your right (incongruously signposted "Cold Drinks" in English) leads to a bar in a stunning location. It is certainly worth spending an hour here in summer,

The steps end in **Gundulićeva Poljana**, which is busy each morning with farmers selling fresh fruit, vegetables and herbs, as well as bottles of lavender oil and strings of dried peppers and figs. At the heart of the square is a statue of Ivan Gundulić (1589–1638), Dubrovnik's greatest poet and a key figure in Croatian literature. The pedestal is decorated with scenes from his poem, *Osman*, describing a victory for the Polish army over the Ottoman Turks.

**5–6**
Turn right beside the statue to emerge on Pred Dvorom

sitting beneath a palm tree on the side of the cliffs and gazing at the isle of Lokrum across the sea.

**4–5**
Keep beside the walls as they bend left beneath the bastion of Sveta Margarita. Looking to your left, you can see the Jesuit Church (Sv. Ignacija) dominating the market square of **Poljana Ruđera Boškovića**. Completed in 1725, this is the largest church in Dubrovnik, its interior a riot of baroque excess with marble altars and mosaic tiles. Cross the square and walk down the monumental Jesuit Steps, built in 1738 to provide a suitably grand approach to the church and based on the Spanish Steps in Rome.

Gradska Luka

Dominikanski Samostan

Sv Nikola

6

Knežev Dvor

PRED DVOROM

Katedrala

Vrata od Buže

7

Pelíne

Žudioska

Luža

Gundulićeva Poljana

Sinagoga

PRIJEKO

5

Puča

Uz Jezuíte

M PERIĆA IZA GRADA

PLACA (STRADUN)

Od

Poljana Ruđera Boškovića

Tvrđava Minčeta

Palmotíćeva

Od Puča

SIROKA

2

Dom Marina Držíća

Sv Ignacija

Pelíne

IZA GRADA

Sv Spasa

8

Čarítíste

Sv Roka

Od Domina

Od Rupa

Etnografskí Muzej Rupe

3

Od Kaštela

Od Margaríte

Vrata od Pile

1

Od Sorte

Samostan Sv Maríje

4

Pile

0    100 metres
0    100 yards

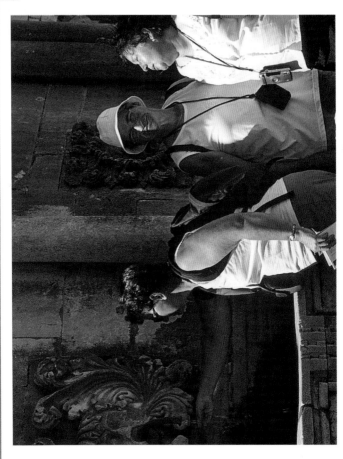

in front of the Rector's Palace (**Knežev Dvor**) with the cathedral to your right, then turn left to reach **Luža**, the broad square which marks the east end of Stradun. Above you is the 15th-century clock tower, heavily rebuilt, with a clock with numerals added in the early 20th century. Peer up to the top of the belfry and you may just be able to make out Maro and Baro reconstructions of the original bronze figures who strike the hours with their hammers. Beneath the tower is a small fountain designed by Onofrio della Cava (▶ 175).

In the middle of the square is another Dubrovnik landmark, the statue of an armoured knight at the foot of the Orlando Column. This remarkably gentle-looking figure is based on the cult of Orlando, the local name for the hero of the French epic poem *Chanson de Roland*. The original Roland was killed in battle in the Pyrenees, but the legend has been reinvented and has him ambushed by Saracens while defending Dubrovnik during the Crusades. During the time of the Ragusan republic, when Dubrovnik was an independent city-state, new laws were proclaimed from

**The Onofrio Fountain, just inside Pile Gate**

the Orlando Column and the statue's right arm was used as a unit of measurement (51.2cm/20 inches).

## 6–7

Turn left along **Stradun** and take the second right onto **Ulica Žudioska**. This was the main street of the 16th-century Jewish ghetto, whose gates were locked each night to keep the Jewish population in. A short way up on the left is the synagogue, which still serves a small Jewish community today and also contains an interesting museum (open summer daily 10–8; winter Mon–Fri 10–3).

At the top of the first flight of steps, you cross over **Prijeko**, the main thoroughfare of the upper town, running parallel to Stradun. Glance to your right to see the little Church of **Sv. Nikola (St Nicholas)** at the end of the street, with the Dominican monastery behind it. Continue climbing to the top of **Ulica Žudioska** to reach Peline.

## 7–8

Now you are in the highest part of town. Turn left along **Peline**, passing the **Buža Gate (Vrata od Buža)**, one of five entrances to the

city. Take the right fork and continue along this street as it clings to the inside of the ramparts on its way to the Minčeta Tower **(Tvrđava Minčeta)**, a two-floor circular fortress. The steep, narrow lanes to your left provide a series of wonderful vistas over the old town and back down to Stradun through a jumble of washing lines, little balconies, winding staircases and pot plants. Turn left along Palmotićeva or any of the other streets to return to Stradun.

### TAKING A BREAK

There are numerous **bars and cafés** in the old town. For a drink with a view on a sunny day, you cannot beat **Buža**, reached through a gap in the city walls. A good spot for people-watching is the terrace of the **Gradskavana**, an old-style café between the clock tower and the Rector's Palace at Pred Dvorom 3. The restaurants along Prijeko are geared up for the tourist trade and mainly serve bland, overpriced food, but an exception is **Rozarij** (► 160–161).

**The Stradun, which runs east–west through the city**

# 5 Lokrum
## Walk

The wooded isle of Lokrum is Dubrovnik's summer garden, where people go to escape the city, to walk, swim and sunbathe, to breathe fresh air and indulge in romantic trysts. A day out on Lokrum makes a relaxing break from sightseeing in Dubrovnik – take a boat to the island and then you can walk around the island in under two hours, but it is best to allow half a day, or bring your towel and swimwear and make a complete day of it.

**DISTANCE** 4km (2.5 miles) plus boat trip **TIME** 2–3 hours
**START/END POINT** Old Harbour, Dubrovnik ⊞ 198 B1

Step ashore at the harbour and climb the ramp beside the jetty. On your right is the old forest ranger's house, destroyed by Serbian shells in 1991 and now left abandoned as a memorial. From here, a well-signed network of walking trails leads across the island.

Take the footpath behind the house and stay on this shady lane as it clings to the northern shore, with occasional tracks through the trees leading to rocky beaches and bathing platforms. When the path forks, keep right above the shore, dropping down to reach the **Cross of Triton**, which commemorates the victims of a shipwreck in 1859.

Bear left above a small jetty and climb into the woods, leaving the shore behind. You soon reach **Lazaret**, the old quarantine hospital, enclosed by high walls designed to prevent infections from spreading.

## THE BOAT TRIP

Boats depart regularly in summer from the Old Harbour in Dubrovnik; check the time of the last boat back (it is usually 6pm). The trip to the island takes about 15 minutes and the cost of the ticket includes admission to Lokrum.

of a botanical garden. Turn left at the corner to walk through a beautiful wild olive grove with glimpses of the sea to your right. The **botanical gardens** are on your left, with numerous varieties of cactus and palm trees and peacocks strutting around. Follow the path around to the right to reach the former

**Boats make the scenic crossing from Dubrovnik to Lokrum regularly**

## THE LOKRUM CURSE

Do not visit Lokrum if you are superstitious. Ever since the 19th century, there has been persistent talk of "the curse of Lokrum", perhaps placed by Benedictine monks in revenge for the destruction of their monastery. One owner, Archduke Maximilian, became emperor of Mexico but was killed by his subjects in 1867; the island later passed to his nephew, Crown Prince Rudolf, who committed suicide in 1889. Today the island is uninhabited and there are few people who would be willing to spend the night there.

Take the path to the right around Lazaret and continue climbing until you come to the highest point of the island, crowned by a ruined French fortress, **Fort Royal**, dating from 1806. You can walk inside the star-shaped fort and climb the spiral staircase to the roof for 360-degree views of Dubrovnik, the whole of Lokrum and the sea as far south as Cavtat (▶ 157).

Leaving Fort Royal, take the path through the trees directly opposite where you entered and drop down towards the middle of the

**Benedictine monastery**. Although much of the building is off limits, you can wander around the dilapidated cloisters, which lead to an ornamental garden with a belvedere looking out to sea. Beyond the monastery, a path heads down to a swimming and sunbathing area. Instead, take the path signposted No 4 to Mrtvo More (Dead Sea). Passing a

island along the Rajski Put (Celestial Way), a processional route lined with tall cypress trees. Reaching a junction, turn right through the pine woods and go down the steps beside a large reservoir, passing around the edge

**View across Lokrum from the French fort**

children's playground, you reach this saltwater lake, connected to the sea by an
underground channel. The water is shallow, so
safe for children and non-swimmers.

Turn left on path No 5 to return to the
monastery on a woodland path, arriving in
the landscaped **Maximilian Gardens**, from
where it is a short stroll back to the harbour.
Alternatively, for a longer walk, a series of
footpaths leads around the wilder southern
shore of the island, dropping down to
Lokrum's popular naturist beach, with its
concrete bathing platforms and dreamy views
across the water to Cavtat.

**TAKING A BREAK**

There is a **restaurant** inside the **monastery
cloisters**, which is open in high summer. At
other times, a **small bar** near the **harbour**
(open summer daily 9–6) sells sandwiches and
cold drinks. A pleasant alternative is to buy
picnic food in Dubrovnik and take it across to
the island.

# Practicalities

## BEFORE YOU GO

### WHAT YOU NEED

| | | UK | Germany | USA | Canada | Australia | Ireland | New Zealand | France |
|---|---|---|---|---|---|---|---|---|---|
| ● Required<br>○ Suggested<br>▲ Not required<br>△ Not applicable | Some countries require a passport to remain valid for a minimum period (usually at least six months) beyond the date of entry – contact their consulate or embassy or your travel agent for details. | | | | | | | | |
| Passport/National Identity Card | | ● | ● | ● | ● | ● | ● | ● | ● |
| Visa (regulations can change – check before booking your trip) | | ▲ | ▲ | ▲ | ▲ | ▲ | ▲ | ▲ | ▲ |
| Onward or Return Ticket | | ○ | ○ | ○ | ○ | ○ | ○ | ○ | ○ |
| Health Inoculations (tetanus and polio) | | ▲ | ▲ | ▲ | ▲ | ▲ | ▲ | ▲ | ▲ |
| Health Documentation | | ▲ | ▲ | ▲ | ▲ | ▲ | ▲ | ▲ | ▲ |
| Travel Insurance | | ○ | ○ | ○ | ○ | ○ | ○ | ○ | ○ |
| Driver's Licence (national) | | ● | ● | ● | ● | ● | ● | ● | ● |
| Car Insurance Certificate | | ● | ● | ● | ● | ● | ● | ● | ● |
| Car Registration Document | | ● | ● | ● | ● | ● | ● | ● | ● |

## WHEN TO GO

High season          Low season

| JAN | FEB | MAR | APR | MAY | JUN | JUL | AUG | SEP | OCT | NOV | DEC |
|---|---|---|---|---|---|---|---|---|---|---|---|
| 11°C | 12°C | 14°C | 17°C | 21°C | 25°C | 28°C | 28°C | 25°C | 21°C | 16°C | 13°C |
| 52°F | 54°F | 57°F | 63°F | 70°F | 77°F | 82°F | 82°F | 77°F | 70°F | 61°F | 55°F |

Sun      Cloud      Wet      Sun/Showers

The temperatures above are the **average daily maximum** for each month on the Adriatic islands and coast. Inland temperatures are considerably lower, often dropping below 0°C in Zagreb and highland areas in winter. Snow is common in the mountains. The sunniest place in Croatia is Hvar Town, which averages more than 2,700 hours of sunshine per year. During the summer months, the sea temperature can be as high as 28°C. The best months to visit are May, June, September and October, when there is less traffic and fewer tourists, but the sea is pleasantly mild. Late spring and early autumn are also good times for sailing and active holidays. The busiest months on the coast are July and August. Many hotels close down altogether between November and March.

### GETTING ADVANCE INFORMATION

**Websites**
■ Croatian National Tourist Board: www.croatia.hr
■ Croatia web portal: www.hr

■ Ministry of Foreign Affairs (for visa information): www.mvpei.hr
■ Jadrolinija (ferry routes and timetables): www.jadrolinija.hr

**In the UK**
Croatian National Tourist Office
2 The Lanchesters
162–164 Fulham Palace Road, London W6 9ER
☎ 020 8563 7979

## GETTING THERE

**By Air** There are **international airports** at Zagreb, Split, Dubrovnik, Pula, Rijeka and Zadar. The national carrier, Croatia Airlines (www.croatiaairlines.hr), has regular flights to Zagreb from major European cities, with additional flights to the coastal airports in summer. Links to North American cities are available through the Star Alliance network. Other airlines flying to Croatia include British Airways, Austrian Airlines and Lufthansa. **Budget airlines** flying to Croatia from the UK include easyJet (www.easyjet.com) to Split, Flybe (www.flybe.com) to Dubrovnik and Split, Ryanair (www.ryanair.com) to Pula and Zadar, and Wizzair (www.wizzair.com) to Zagreb. There are also numerous **charter flights** from British and European cities in summer. Most seats on charter flights are allocated to tour operators, but flight-only deals are sometimes available online.

**By Sea** Jadrolinija (www.jadrolinija.hr) operates **car and passenger ferries** between Italy and Croatia. The main routes are Ancona to Split, Ancona to Zadar and Bari to Dubrovnik, as well as the Adriatic coastal route linking Dubrovnik with Korčula, Stari Grad, Split and Rijeka. Foot passengers can generally buy tickets at the quayside, but car passengers should book in advance. Ferries from Italy to Croatia are also operated by SEM Marina (www.splittours.hr) and SNAV (www.snav.it). In summer, Venezia Lines (www.venezialines.com) and Emilia Romagna (www.emiliaromagnalines.it) operate high-speed links from Venice, Rimini and Ravenna to the Istrian coast.

**By Land** Croatia shares **land borders** with Slovenia, Hungary, Bosnia-Hercegovina, Serbia and Montenegro. There are **bus and rail links** from Zagreb to most major European cities.

## TIME

Croatia is on Central European Time, one hour ahead of Greenwich Mean Time. Summer time (GMT+2) operates from the last Sunday in March to the last Sunday in October.

## CURRENCY AND FOREIGN EXCHANGE

**Currency** Croatia's currency is the **kuna (kn)**, named after the pine-marten, whose fur was once used for trading. The kuna is divided into 100 lipa. Coins are issued in denominations of 1, 2, 5, 10, 20 and 50 lipa, 1kn, 2kn and 5kn. Notes are issued in denominations of 5, 10, 20, 50, 100, 200, 500 and 1,000kn. The **euro (€)** is widely accepted at hotels and many prices in tourist hotels are quoted in both euros and kuna.

**Exchange** Foreign currency and travellers' cheques can be changed at banks, travel agencies and hotels. You will need to show your passport when cashing travellers' cheques. You can also withdraw cash from ATM (cashpoint) machines in all towns and cities using your credit or debit card with a PIN (personal identification number). Your own bank will usually make a charge for this service.

**Credit cards** Major credit cards are widely accepted, though it is always advisable to have some cash. Be aware that restaurants outside the cities often do not accept cards.

**In the US**
Croatian National
Tourist Office
350 Fifth Avenue,
Suite 4003
New York, NY 10118
☎ 212/279-8672

**In France**
Croatian National
Tourist Office
Avenue Victor Hugo 48
75116 Paris
☎ 01 45 00 99 55

**In Germany**
Croatian National
Tourist Office
Kaiserstrasse 23
60311 Frankfurt
☎ 069 238 5350

## WHEN YOU ARE THERE

### CLOTHING SIZES

| UK | Croatia/Europe | USA | |
|---|---|---|---|
| 36 | 46 | 36 | |
| 38 | 48 | 38 | |
| 40 | 50 | 40 | Suits |
| 42 | 52 | 42 | |
| 44 | 54 | 44 | |
| 46 | 56 | 46 | |
| 7 | 41 | 8 | |
| 7.5 | 42 | 8.5 | |
| 8.5 | 43 | 9.5 | Shoes |
| 9.5 | 44 | 10.5 | |
| 10.5 | 45 | 11.5 | |
| 11 | 46 | 12 | |
| 14.5 | 37 | 14.5 | |
| 15 | 38 | 15 | |
| 15.5 | 39/40 | 15.5 | Shirts |
| 16 | 41 | 16 | |
| 16.5 | 42 | 16.5 | |
| 17 | 43 | 17 | |
| 8 | 34 | 6 | |
| 10 | 36 | 8 | |
| 12 | 38 | 10 | Dresses |
| 14 | 40 | 12 | |
| 16 | 42 | 14 | |
| 18 | 44 | 16 | |
| 4.5 | 38 | 6 | |
| 5 | 38 | 6.5 | |
| 5.5 | 39 | 7 | Shoes |
| 6 | 39 | 7.5 | |
| 6.5 | 40 | 8 | |
| 7 | 41 | 0.5 | |

### NATIONAL HOLIDAYS

| 1 Jan | New Year's Day |
|---|---|
| 6 Jan | Epiphany |
| Mar/Apr | Easter Monday |
| 1 May | Labour Day |
| May/Jun | Corpus Christi |
| 22 Jun | Anti-Fascist Resistance Day |
| 25 Jun | Croatian National Day |
| 5 Aug | Victory Day |
| 15 Aug | Feast of the Assumption |
| 8 Oct | Independence Day |
| 1 Nov | All Saints' Day |
| 25–26 Dec | Christmas |

### OPENING HOURS

○ Shops  ● Post Offices
● Offices  ● Museums/Monuments
● Banks  ● Pharmacies

8am 9am 10am noon 1pm 2pm 4pm 5pm 7pm

☐ Day  ☐ Midday  ☐ Evening

**Shops** Most are closed on Saturday afternoon and all day Sunday. Some close for a break on weekday afternoons. Shopping centres in Zagreb, and shops in coastal resorts in summer, may stay open for longer hours and on Sundays.
**Banks** Generally open Mon–Fri 7–7, Sat 7–1.
**Museums** Opening hours vary widely, and it's best to consult the individual listings in this book. Many are closed on Mondays and weekend afternoons.
**Pharmacies** In larger towns, there will usually be a duty pharmacy open at night and weekends.
**Post offices** Main post offices are open Mon–Fri 7–7, Sat 7–1. Post offices in larger towns and cities stay open till 10pm.

### TIME DIFFERENCES

| GMT | Croatia | USA New York | Germany | Spain | Australia |
|---|---|---|---|---|---|
| 12 noon | 1pm | 7am | 1pm | 1pm | Sydney 10pm |

## PERSONAL SAFETY

- Do not leave valuables on the beach or poolside.
- Always lock valuables in hotel safety deposit boxes.
- Never leave anything inside your car. If you have to, lock it out of sight in the boot.
- Beware of pickpockets in crowded markets, and on buses and trams in Split, Dubrovnik and Zagreb.
- Avoid discussions of the recent war, especially in ethnic Serb areas close to the Bosnian and Serbian borders.
- Stick to marked footpaths in remote border areas, and pay close attention to landmine warning signs.

**Police assistance:**
☎ 92 from any phone

## TELEPHONES

logo. Mobile phone coverage is almost universal; the main network operators are T-Com and VIP. Make sure your phone is switched to international roaming before you go. The international dialling code for Croatia is 385.

There are public telephones in all main towns. Phonecards *(telefonska kartica)* can be bought from post offices, news kiosks and shops with the HT (Hrvatski Telekom)

**International Dialling Codes**
**Dial 00 followed by**

| | |
|---|---|
| UK: | 44 |
| USA /Canada: | 1 |
| Irish Republic: | 353 |
| Australia: | 61 |
| Germany: | 49 |

## POST

Stamps can be bought at post offices and news kiosks. Postboxes are yellow and marked HP. Letters to EU countries generally arrive within 5 to 10 days, and to the US within two weeks. For urgent mail, use internet cafés in the main towns and resorts.

## ELECTRICITY

The power supply is 220 volts AC. Sockets take two-pronged round continental plugs. Visitors from the UK will need an adaptor and visitors from the USA will need a transformer for 100–120 volt devices.

## TIPS/GRATUITIES

Tipping is not expected for all services and rates are generally lower than elsewhere.

| | |
|---|---|
| Restaurants | 10 per cent |
| Taxis | 10 per cent |
| Tour guides | 10–20kn |
| Porters | 10kn |
| Chambermaids | 10kn per night |
| Toilet attendants | No |

**POLICE 92**

**FIRE 93**

**AMBULANCE 94**

## HEALTH

 **Insurance** Citizens of EU countries receive free emergency medical treatment on production of their passport under a reciprocal health care agreement. This covers essential hospital stays, but excludes some expenses such as the cost of prescribed medicines. Private medical insurance is still advised and is essential for all other visitors.

 **Dental Services** Dental treatment has to be paid for by all visitors, but is usually covered by private medical insurance.

 **Sun** The sun is intense on the Adriatic coast in summer and you can burn very quickly. Cover up with a high-factor sunscreen, wear a hat and drink plenty of water. Children are especially vulnerable and need to be protected, especially near the sea.

 **Drugs** Prescription and non-prescription drugs and medicines are available from pharmacies *(ljekarna)*. Outside normal hours, a notice on pharmacy doors gives the address of the nearest duty chemist. Take adequate supplies of any drugs you need regularly as they may not be available. Other items to consider include insect repellent, anti-diarrhoea pills and sea-sickness tablets if you are going to be using the ferries.

 **Safe Water** Tap water is safe to drink. Bottled mineral water is widely available.

## CONCESSIONS

**Young People** Children under 12 pay half-price on most buses, trains and ferries, while children under three go free. An international student identity card (ISIC) gives discounts at museums and on public transport.
**Senior Citizens** Travellers over 60 may be entitled to discounted admission at museums and reduced fares on public transport.

## TRAVELLING WITH A DISABILITY

Croatia has made great strides in providing facilities for travellers with disabilities, following a war in which many Croatians were disabled, but many older buildings are still inaccessible and cobbled streets in Dubrovnik and Zagreb are a particular problem for wheelchairs. Most modern hotels are suitable for disabled visitors. Before booking a holiday, discuss your particular needs with a tour operator or hotel.

## CHILDREN

Hotels and restaurants are generally very child-friendly, and many hotels and campsites have playgrounds and children's pools. Most beaches are rocky rather than sandy, so plastic sandals are a good idea.

## TOILETS

Public toilets can be found at bus and train stations. They usually make a small charge.

## CUSTOMS

The import of wildlife souvenirs from rare and endangered species may be illegal or require a special permit. Before buying, check your home country's customs regulations.

## CONSULATES AND EMBASSIES

 **UK** ☎ 01 6009 100

 **USA** ☎ 01 6612 200

 **Ireland** ☎ 01 6310 025

 **Australia** ☎ 01 4891 200

 **New Zealand** ☎ 01 4612 060

## LANGUAGE

The official language of Croatia is Croatian (*hrvatski*). Until 1991, this was known as Serbo-Croat, but it is now recognized as a separate language. Unlike Serbian, which uses the Cyrillic script, Croatian uses the Latin alphabet, though otherwise many words are identical. Croatian is entirely phonetic, which means that every word is pronounced exactly as it is written. Additional letters used in Croatian are č (pronounced 'ch'), ć (almost the same), š (pronouned 'sh'), ž (pronounced like a 'j') and đ (pronouned 'dj'). The letter 'c' is pronounced 'ts' and 'j' is pronounced 'y'.

## GENERAL

hi **bog**
hello/good day **dobar dan**
good morning **dobro jutro**
good evening **dobra večer**
goodbye **dovi'enja**
how are you? **kako ste**
please **molim**
thank you **hvala**
excuse me **oprostite**
yes **da**
no **ne**
here you are **izvolite**
cheers! **živjeli!**
large **veliko**
small **malo**
cheap **jeftin**
expensive **skupo**
Croatia **hrvatska**
America **amerika**
England **engleska**
I don't understand **ne razumijem**
do you speak English? **govorite li engleski?**
open **otvoreno**
closed **zatvoreno**
excuse me **izvinite**

tourist office **turistički ured**
embassy **veleposlanstvo**
consulate **konzulami ured**
cathedral **katedrala**
church **crkva**
garden **vrt**
library **knjižnica**
doctor **liječnik/doktor**
dentist **zubar**
police **policija**
hospital **bolnica**
entrance **ulaz**
exit **izlaz**

## ACCOMMODATION

hotel **hotel**
room **soba**
single room **jednokrevetna soba**
double room **dvokrevetna soba**
apartment **apartman**
bath **kupaona**
shower **tuš**
toilet **zahod**
balcony **balkon**
telephone **telefon**
television **televizor**
breakfast **doručak**
half-board **polupansion**
key **ključ**
reservation **rezervacija**
campsite **autokamp**

## RESTAURANT

restaurant **restauracija**
inn **konoba**
café **kavana**
cake shop **slastičarnica**
breakfast **doručak**
lunch **ručak**
dinner **večeru**
menu **jelovnik**
wine list **vinska karta**
the bill **račun**

## NUMBERS

| | | | | | | | |
|---|---|---|---|---|---|---|---|
| 0 | **nula** | 10 | **deset** | 20 | **dvadeset** | 200 | **dvjesto** |
| 1 | **jedan** | 11 | **jedanaest** | 30 | **trideset** | 300 | **tristo** |
| 2 | **dva** | 12 | **dvanaest** | 40 | **četrdeset** | 400 | **četristo** |
| 3 | **tri** | 13 | **trinaest** | 50 | **pedeset** | 500 | **petsto** |
| 4 | **četiri** | 14 | **četrnaest** | 60 | **šezdeset** | 600 | **šeststo** |
| 5 | **pet** | 15 | **petnaest** | 70 | **sedamdeset** | 700 | **sedamsto** |
| 6 | **šest** | 16 | **šestnaest** | 80 | **osamdeset** | 800 | **osamsto** |
| 7 | **sedam** | 17 | **sedamnaest** | 90 | **devedeset** | 900 | **devetsto** |
| 8 | **osam** | 18 | **osamnaest** | 100 | **sto** | 1000 | **tisuću** |
| 9 | **devet** | 19 | **devetnaest** | 101 | **sto i jedan** | | |

## TRANSPORT

bus **autobus**
tram **tramvaj**
train **vlak**
bus station **autobusni kolodvor**
train station **zeljeznički kolodvor**
airport **zračna luka**
port **luka**
ferry **trajekt**
ticket **karta**
timetable **vozni red**
arrival **dolazak**
departure **odlazak**
taxi **taksi**
petrol **benzin**

## MONEY

bank **banka**
exchange **razmjena**
exchange rate **tečaj**
cashier **blagajnik**
money **novac**
cash **gotovina**
banknote **novčanice**
coin **kovani novac**
credit card **kreditna karta**
travellers' cheque **travel čekove**
post office **pošta**
stamp **poštanske marka**
postcard **razglednica**
telephone card **telekarta**

## SHOPPING

bakery **pekara**
bookshop **knjižara**
butchers **mesnica**
cake shop **slastičarna**
pharmacy **ljekarna**
market **tržnica**
travel agent **putnička agencija**

## TIME

hour **sat**
minute **minuta**
week **tjedan**
day **dan**
today **danas**
tomorrow **sutra**
yesterday **jučer**

## MENU READER

**barbun** red mullet
**bijelo vino** white wine
**blitva** Swiss chard
**breskva** peach
**brudet** fish stew
**čaj** tea
**čaj sa limunom** tea with lemon
**čevapčići** spicy meatballs
**crni rižot** black risotto
**crno vino** red wine
**češnjak** garlic
**cipal** grey mullet
**dagnje** mussels
**divlja svinija** wild boar
**džem** jam
**riš paprikaš** spicy fish stew
**gazirana mineralna voda** sparkling mineral water
**govedina** beef
**grah** beans
**grčka** cheese

**grgeč** perch
**gulaš** goulash
**jabuka** apple
**jaje (jaja)** egg (eggs)
**janjetina** lamb
**jastog** lobster
**juha** soup
**kajmak** clotted sour cream
**kava** coffee
**krastavac** cucumber
**kruh** bread
**krumpir** potatoes
**kruške** pears
**kulen** spicy salami
**kupus** cabbage
**lignje** squid
**limun** lemon
**losos** salmon trout
**lozovača** brandy
**luben** bass
**luk** onion
**marelica** apricot
**maslinovo ulje** olive oil
**meso** meat
**mješana salata** mixed salad

**musaka** moussaka
**naranča** orange
**negazarina mineralna voda** still mineral water
**njoki** gnocchi
**ocat** vinegar
**oštrige** oysters
**ovčetina** mutton
**palačinke** pancakes
**papar** pepper
**paprike** green peppers
**paški sir** sheep's cheese
**pašticada** beef with dumplings
**pastrva** trout
**piletina** chicken
**pomfrit** chips
**pršut** smoked ham
**ragu** thick soup
**rajčica** tomato
**rak** crab
**rakija** spirit
**ramsteak** rump steak

**riba** fish
**riža** rice
**roze vino** rosé wine
**sardina** sardines
**sarma** stuffed cabbage or vine leaves
**sir** cheese
**škampi** crayfish
**sladoled** ice-cream
**slan** salt
**špinat** spinach
**šunka** ham
**svinjetina** pork
**tartufi** truffles
**teletina** veal
**travarica** spirit flavoured with herbs
**tuna** tuna
**ulje** oil
**voće** fruits
**voda** water
**zelena** lettuce
**zelena salata** green salad
**zubatac** bream

To identify the regions, see the map on
the inside of the front cover

## Regional Maps

▬▬▬ Major route
░░░ Motorway
░░░ National road
░░░ Regional road
– – – International boundary
    National Park
░░░ Built up area

◼ Featured place of interest
◼ Place of interest
▲ Height in metres
▢▫ City/town
✈ Airport

192–199

## Streetplans

═══ Main road / minor road
─── Railway
◼ Featured place of interest
✝ Church

▨ Important building
    Park/garden
ℹ Tourist Information
⊓⊔ City walls

200/201

202

# Atlas

ZELENGAJ

Novi Goljak

Kozarčeva

Goljak

PANTOVČAK

Zelengaj

Jabukovac

TUSKANAC

Knežin Gvozd

Tuškanac

JURJEVSKA

Dubravkin put

Zamehoffova

VLADIMIRA NAZORA

Ivana Gorana Kovačića

Golubovac

Muzej
Grada
Zagreba

Stjepana Radića

Radićeva

Opatička

Demetrova

Fondacija
Ivan Meštrović

Prirodoslovni
Muzej

Markov
trg

Visoka

Mesnička

Matoševa

Sv.
Marka

Sabor

Kam.

Habdelić

Kamen
Vrata

Hrvatski Muzej
Naivne Umjetnosti

Kula Lotršćak

Katarinin
Trg

Sv.
Katerina

I Kukuljevica

PANTOVČAK

Pavlinoviceva

Bulatova

Rokova

Dežmanova

Strossm. Šetalište

Tomiceva

Uspinjača

Buconjičeva

Arnoldova

ILICA

ILICA

Britanski
trg

ILICA

Trg Petra
Preradovića

Bogovićeva

Kordunska

Medulićeva

Dalmatin.

Frankopanska

Varšavska

Gundulićeva

N TESLE

PRILAZ GYURE DEŽELIĆA

MASARYKOVA

P. Preradovića

Berislav

Hochmanova

KLAIČEVA

Trg Maršala
Tita

Muzej Za
Umjetnost i Obrt

Hrvatsko
Narodno
Kazalište

A HEBRANGA

JAGIĆEVA

MAGAZINSKA

Andrije Žaje

Božidara Adžije

Muzej
Mimara

Rooseveltov
trg

Mažuranićev
trg

Etnografski
Muzej

DONJI GRAD

J ŽERJAVIĆA

BARUNA

Gundulićeva

Haulikova

Za
Ka
Lu

JUKIĆEVA

BROZOTA

KRŠRJAGOVA

SAVSKA CESTA

Marulićev
trg

KUMIĆEVA

MIHANO

VODNIKOVA

Runjan

Botanički vrt

Crnatkova

Bednjanska

MIRAMARSKA

Tehnički
Muzej

KRANJČEVIĆEVA

Badalićeva

TRATINSKA

SAVSKA CESTA

Koturaška

Koturaška

Surjanska

Unska

HORVATOVAC

Horvatovac
Zeleni dol
Zelenjak
Horvatovac
Čačkovićeva
Wickenhauserova
Babonićeva
Mikulićeva

Milinarska
Žnikina
Šuflaja
M
Groblje Mirogoj, Medvednica

Nova Ves
MEDVEŠČAK
GRŠKOVIĆA
Suhinova
Torbarova
Dvorničeva
Vinkovićeva
Galdekova
Mešićeva
Šalata

Medvedgradska
Miklou-šićeva
Trakošćeva
Degenova
Weberova
Vramčeva
ŠALATA
VOĆARSKA CESTA
VONČININA

KAPTOL
RIBNJAK
Novakova
Šalata
Voćarsko naselje
Jurkovićeva
PETROVA

Opatovina
hita
kaptol
SOŠTARIĆEVA
Rubetićeva
Maksimirski Perivoj

GORNJI GRAD
Trg A Stepinca
Katedrala
BRANJUGOVA
Vlaška
VLAŠKA
Laginjina
3

Dolac
Vlaška
Bakačeva
Cesarčeva
i
J DRAŠKOVIĆA
Iblerov Trg
Smičiklasova
MARTIĆEVA
ANTUNA BAUERA
Vojnovićeva
Barčićeva

Pod zidom
Trg Bana Jelačića
JURIŠIĆEVA
PALMOTIĆEVA
F RAČKOG
Patač-ćeva
Tomaš
Bulić
Lopašićeva
Brešćenskog

PRAŠKA
AMRUŠEVA
Petrinjska
Dordićeva
KRALJA ZVONIMIRA
Staneićeva

Arheološki Muzej
ičeva
Trg Nikole Šubića Zrinskog
R BOŠKOVIĆA
K DRŽISLAVA
Trg Hrvatskih Velikana
KNEZA VIŠESLAVA
K L Posav.
2

Strossmayerova Galerija Starih Majstora
Strossm. trg
Mrazović
J DRAŠKOVIĆA
K MISLAVA
Križanićeva
Švear
Kružićeva

Galeva
TRENKA
P HATZA
Petrinjska
Kneza
Borne
Hrvoj.
K Jelene
Erdödyeva
Domagojeva
Trpimirova

grebačko
izalište
taka
Trg kralja Tomislava
Palmotićeva
A Šenoina

OVIĆEVA
Grgurova
KNEZA BRANIMIRA
Autobusni kolodvor
Strojarska cesta

ŽELJEZNIČKA STANICA
Strojarska cesta

Paromlinska
Trnjanska cesta
Koncertna Dvorana Vatrolava Lisinskog
Trg Stjepan Radica

# Dubrovnik

## Zagreb

## Picture credits

The Automobile Association would like to thank the following photographers, companies and picture libraries for their assistance in the preparation of this book.

Abbreviations for the picture credits are as follows – (t) top; (b) bottom; (c) centre; (l) left; (r) right; (AA) AA World Travel Library.

2i AA/P Bennett; 2ii AA/P Bennett; 2iii AA/P Bennett; 2iv AA/P Bennett; 2v AA/P Bennett; 3i AA/P Bennett; 3ii AA/P Bennett; 3iii AA/P Bennett; 5l AA/P Bennett; 5bl AA/P Bennett; 5br A/N Setchfield, 7 AA/P Bennett; 8/9 Gabriel Bouys/AFP/Getty Images; 10l AA/P Bennett; 10r AA/P Bennett; 11 AA/P Bennett; 12 AA/P Bennett; 14 AA/P Bennett; 16 AA/J Smith; 17 AA/J Smith; 18 AA/J Smith; 19bg AA/P Bennett; 19t AA/P Bennett; 19c AA/P Bennett; 19b AA/P Bennett; 20/21bg AA/P Bennett; 20/21 AA/P Bennett; 22t AA/P Bennett; 22b AA/P Bennett; 23t AA/P Bennett; 23b AA/P Bennett; 24 Photodisc; 25 Staffan Widstrand/naturepl.com; 26 Regional Tourist Board Dubrovnik Riviera and Islands; 27 Regional Tourist Board Dubrovnik Riviera and Islands; 29 © allOver Photography/Alamy; 30 © Hrvoje Polan/AFP/Getty Images; 31l AA/P Bennett; 31bl AA/P Bennett; 31br AA/P Bennett; 41l AA/P Bennett; 41bl AA/P Bennett; 41br AA/P Bennett; 43 AA/P Bennett; 44t AA/P Bennett; 44b AA/P Bennett; 45 AA/P Bennett; 46 AA/P Bennett; 47 AA/P Bennett; 48 AA/P Bennett; 49 AA/P Bennett; 50/51 AA/P Bennett; 52 AA/P Bennett; 53 AA/P Bennett; 54 AA/P Bennett; 55 AA/P Bennett; 56 AA/P Bennett; 57 AA/P Bennett; 59 Françoise De Mulder/Roger-Viollet; 65l AA/P Bennett; 65bl AA/P Bennett; 65br AA/P Bennett; 66/67 AA/P Bennett; 68t AA/P Bennett; 68b AA/P Bennett; 69 Pete Bennett; 71 AA/P Bennett; 72 AA/P Bennett; 73 AA/P Bennett; 74 AA/P Bennett; 75 AA/P Bennett; 76 AA/P Bennett; 78 AA/P Bennett; 80 AA/P Bennett; 81 AA/P Bennett; 82 AA/P Bennett; 83 AA/P Bennett; 84 AA/P Bennett; 89l AA/P Bennett; 89bl AA/P Bennett; 89br AA/P Bennett; 91 AA/P Bennett; 92 AA/P Bennett; 93t AA/P Bennett; 93b AA/P Bennett; 94 AA/P Bennett; 96 AA/P Bennett; 97 AA/P Bennett; 98 AA/P Bennett; 99 Croatian Tourist Board; 100 © Sipa Press/Rex Features; 101 Croatian Tourist Board; 102 AA/P Bennett; 103 AA/P Bennett; 104 AA/P Bennett; 105 AA/P Bennett; 106t AA/P Bennett; 106b AA/P Bennett; 107 AA/P Bennett; 113l AA/P Bennett; 113bl AA/J Smith; 113br AA/J Smith; 115 AA/P Bennett; 116 AA/P Bennett; 117 AA/P Bennett; 118 AA/P Bennett; 119 AA/P Bennett; 120 © Photographers Choice/Connie Coleman/Getty Images; 121 AA/P Bennett; 122 Gavin Heller/Robert Harding; 123 AA/P Bennett; 124 AA/P Bennett; 125 AA/P Bennett; 126/127 AA/P Bennett; 128 AA/P Bennett; 129 AA/P Bennett; 130/131 AA/P Bennett; 132 Pete Bennett; 134 AA/P Bennett; 135 AA/P Bennett; 136 AA/P Bennett; 141l AA/P Bennett; 141bl AA/J Smith; 141br AA/P Bennett; 142 AA/P Bennett; 143 AA/P Bennett; 144 AA/P Bennett; 145t © Diomedia/Alamy; 145b AA/P Bennett; 147 AA/P Bennett; 148 AA/P Bennett; 150 © Nelly Boyd/Alamy; 151 Croatian Tourist Board; 152 AA/P Bennett; 154 AA/P Bennett; 155 AA/P Bennett; 156 AA/P Bennett; 163l AA/P Bennett; 163bl AA/P Bennett; 163br AA/J Smith; 164 AA/P Bennett; 166 AA/P Bennett; 167 AA/P Bennett; 169 AA/P Bennett; 170 AA/P Bennett; 171 AA/P Bennett; 173 AA/P Bennett; 174 AA/J Smith; 175 AA/P Bennett; 176 AA/P Bennett; 178 AA/P Bennett; 179 AA/P Bennettl 181 AA/P Bennett; 182 AA/P Bennett; 183l AA/P Bennett; 183bl AA/T Kelly; 183br AA/P Bennett; 187t AA/J Smith; 187bl AA/P Bennett; 187br AA/P Bennett

Every effort has been made to trace the copyright holders, and we apologise in advance for any accidental errors. We would be happy to apply the corrections in the following edition of this publication.

# **SPIRAL**GUIDE
# Questionnaire

## Dear Traveller

Your comments, opinions and recommendations are very important to us. Please help us to improve our travel guides by taking a few minutes to complete this simple questionnaire.

You do not need a stamp (unless posted outside the UK). If you do not want to remove this page from your guide, then photocopy it or write your answers on a plain sheet of paper.

**Send to: The Editor, Spiral Guides, AA World Travel Guides, FREEPOST SCE 4598, Basingstoke RG21 4GY.**

## Your recommendations...

We always encourage readers' recommendations for restaurants, night-life or shopping – if your recommendation is used in the next edition of the guide, we will send you a FREE AA Spiral Guide of your choice. Please state below the establishment name, location and your reasons for recommending it.

_____

_____

_____

_____

_____

**Please send me AA Spiral** _____
(see list of titles inside the back cover)

## About this guide...

Which title did you buy?

_____ **AA Spiral**

Where did you buy it? _____

When? m m / y y

Why did you choose an AA Spiral Guide? _____

_____

_____

_____

Did this guide meet your expectations?

Exceeded ☐   Met all ☐   Met most ☐   Fell below ☐

Please give your reasons _____

_____

_____

_____

_____

continued on next page...

Were there any aspects of this guide that you particularly liked?

_____
_____
_____
_____
_____

Is there anything we could have done better?

_____
_____
_____
_____

## About you...

Name (Mr/Mrs/Ms) _____

Address _____

_____ Postcode _____

Daytime tel no _____ email _____

Please *only* give us your email address and mobile phone number if you wish to hear from us about other products and services from the AA and partners by email or text or mms.

Which age group are you in?

Under 25 ☐   25–34 ☐   35–44 ☐   45–54 ☐   55–64 ☐   65+ ☐

How many trips do you make a year?

Less than one ☐   One ☐   Two ☐   Three or more ☐

Are you an AA member? Yes ☐   No ☐

## About your trip...

When did you book? m m / y y      When did you travel? m m / y y

How long did you stay? _____

Was it for business or leisure? _____

Did you buy any other travel guides for your trip? ☐ Yes ☐ No

If yes, which ones? _____
_____

**Thank you for taking the time to complete this questionnaire. Please send it to us as soon as possible, and remember, you do not need a stamp (unless posted outside the UK).**